From Bitter Came Sweet

'My Journey to the Abode of Supreme Peace'

Ruth Grant

mrivanuk@yahoo.co.uk

Cover design, text layout and design by K.R. Mohan Kumar

Co-Published by
Message Publications

Typeset in **10.5 Arial**

First printing, September 2004
ISBN 81-87694-09-2

Printed and bound in India by Vishruti Prints

THIS BOOK IS DEDICATED
WITH LOVE DEVOTION AND GRATITUDE
TO SRI SATHYA SAI BABA

"There is only one religion, the religion of love
There is only one language, the language of the heart
There is only one caste, the caste of humanity
There is only one God, and He is Omnipresent

Sai Baba

CONTENTS

PART 3

THE ROSE

As this book began to take shape and looked more like a reality than a dream, I wondered what drawing or picture would be appropriate for the front cover. For a while I could not come up with anything that would encompass both the bitter and the sweet. Suddenly, discussing it with a dear friend, he suggested that a Rose with thorns would fit the story well. I began to look for the right type of Rose but it was difficult to find. As I looked in my drawer for a Sai Baba photograph to give to someone, I came across a greeting card with a beautiful white open rose, with a bud and thorns, with gentle healing colours in the background. It was a watercolour by the artist June Lockhart. Immediately I knew it was what I was looking for, the white symbolising purity, and the bud representing the spiritual seed, and the thorns, the pain and suffering. The open petals evoked spiritual enfoldment. How fitting and appropriate it was. I am grateful to June for giving me permission to use her drawing on the cover of this book.

"Make your life a rose that speaks silently the language of fragrance"

Sri Sathya Sai Baba

15.10-2019

To dear Ray
and Sue
with love and
all blessings
Ruth
xx

If I Have Everything

And Yet Do Not Have God - I Have Nothing

If I Have Nothing

But Have God - I Have Everything

Ruth Grant

ABOUT THE AUTHOR

Ruth was born in Tel-Aviv, Israel on the 14th July 1928. It was then Palestine under the British Mandate. After a sad and traumatic childhood, she entered into an arranged marriage on the 30th September 1945 at the early age of 17. Her husband was born in Alexandria, Egypt and joined the Royal Air Force during the Second World War. After their marriage they lived in Cairo, Egypt (1945-1948). On 12th September 1948 her first daughter (Diana) was born during the Arab/Israeli war. Soon after the end of that war they left as refugees via Italy, back to the State of Israel.

Life was tough there after the war. Food was rationed, jobs almost non-existent. Following a year and a half of hardship, they left with very little money for France, where they stayed for six months with her brother-in-law near Paris. Her husband was unable to find work in France, so they moved to England in 1952. After many years of struggle and hard work, they finally reached a stage of affluence, but it was during this time, in 1961, that Ruth had a serious car accident at the age of 33. This became a turning point in her life. In spite of all this, she emerged from the traumatic, mental, physical and emotional scarring caused by the tragedy. First she had to heal herself before she was able to help others. This she did, with remarkable courage and determination, even though at the time she also had to care for her two small daughters. She was told then that she possessed the gift of healing, which has played a significant part in her life, helping many others from 1976 to this day.

AUTHOR'S NOTE

When tragedy and trauma struck in 1961, I had an irresistible inner urge to make notes of my experiences, moods and feelings. Some of these experiences came in dreams and visions; some were 'messages' received through my mind. They were so moving, uplifting, and comforting that I felt compelled to keep a record of them.

When I contemplated what I was receiving, I realised that these were healing words of courage and hope which came from another dimension, which I now know to be our God-selves – the silent voice of the God within – answering my anguished pleas.

I never dreamt that one day all these fragmented notes would come together in a book. Although I felt at times that perhaps all I had written and experienced could be of help to someone, I had no idea how to put it together in the form of a book. It was a task, which I felt, was beyond me, and I pushed it to the back of my mind. Yet the idea was constantly within me. Finally I accepted that 'someone' was telling me to get on with writing the book, and so I could no longer ignore that 'message'.

However, it was not until 1991 that I came to know of Sathya Sai Baba – Saint, Avatar (an incarnation of God on Earth), a world teacher that I began to realise and experience His divine powers. I have read about and spoken to many devotees who have been guided and helped by Baba in work problems or assignments, which they felt totally incapable of accomplishing on their own. Knowing this, I wrote to Baba asking Him for help, guidance and inspiration. I pleaded with Him to send me someone to help organise and mould all my scattered notes into a book format. I had to wait almost three years before that 'someone' came along. From then on others followed. Whatever was needed came just at the right time. Thus the book became a reality and not just a dream.

God is the creator and director of the whole Universe. We are His instruments carrying out the duties He has assigned to us. I am infinitely privileged and blessed to be able to fulfil this task. I hope that those who are seeking may find something in my story that will awaken the spiritual seed within them and enlarge their understanding.

ACKNOWLEDGEMENTS

I express deep gratitude and appreciation to my first spiritual Master of 30 years, Paramahansa Yogananda. His teachings have been the preparation which led me to the Master of Masters, Universal Teacher and Avatar, - Sri Sathya Sai Baba.

I express deep gratitude also to my dearest and most loved friend, Marguerite Burgess, who was the 'someone' sent to help me in the difficult assignment of organising those fragmented bits of papers, encouraging me to write this book, and always giving me, selflessly and lovingly, her wholehearted support. She made me 'take the plunge'. I must truly say that, without her dedicated help from the start, this book would never have seen the light of day.

My heartfelt thanks to my dearest friends Elaine James, for painstakingly proof reading the book and for her continued help and support throughout, and to Sharon Beitler and Kiran Mistry for their help and encouragement.

One morning when nothing was going right, I received a phone call and heard an unfamiliar voice say, "Ruth, I was told you need help with your computer to finish your book. I am free and can come to help!" Being a computer programmer, the owner of the voice was able to provide all the technical assistance, which was needed, working tirelessly and selflessly for three weeks. I do not have words enough to thank this 'angel', who modestly does not want me to mention his name.

Last but not least, I thank a second 'angel', my beloved grandson Alex, who came to stay with me, quite unexpectedly, just at the right time to put onto the computer more additions and corrections over many weeks of a labour of love.

It is my sincere hope that my children and grandchildren, through this book, may see and understand another side of their mother and grandmother.

I acknowledge my debt to those Divine Masters who have come to walk amongst us, at much needed times, to light the lamp of love, peace and truth in the hearts of those who are ready to be awakened, so that we may realise our oneness with our Creator, and thus all life.

FOREWORD

Ruth Grant is an unusual person. Her story is well-worth reading, a travelogue of the spirit, a journey through Israel, Egypt, France and England, through affluence and poverty, through desperate illness, marriage breakdown, rejection of all kinds, a journey from which she emerged, smiling, confident and full of love.

Ruth is a woman who gives of herself. Others, less sensitive, take advantage of the givers of this world. She has suffered as a result. But instead of creating despair and bitterness, her outlook is supremely positive, reflected in the wonderful healing she has given to so many, and the warm friendships she has created.

Her spiritual journey, begun after a devastating accident, passed through many phases until coming to rest in the ashram of Sai Baba. He has clearly been the greatest inspiration in her life, reflecting the same spiritual and moral qualities that inspired her famous rabbinical forebears.

I am privileged to have been asked to add my name to this remarkable story set out in such detail.

Those who have suffered, and those who have not, can derive both comfort and inspiration from this story of one woman's journey through life.

Aubrey Rose C.B.E. D. Univ.

There are more things in heaven and earth, Horatio, than are dreamt of in your philosophy

Hamlet, William Shakespeare

Have you ever wondered whether life's experiences, come about by 'accident', are a 'coincidence', or is it a question of 'good' or 'bad' luck? Is there something deeper to look for, to understand, and to learn from the experiences we have to face?

It is easier by far to blame circumstances, "the world" or someone else for our misfortune, than to try and look deep within and ask some honest questions – to be objective with regard to oneself and the situation. This is the crucial moment, which will determine our attitude to tragedy or trauma, how we are going to deal with it, and where it is going to lead us. The choice is entirely within oneself, to discover a positive attitude and path leading to self-knowledge, finding the strength within, rather than to shrink into self-pity, resentment and bitterness.

This was the choice I had to make on 11th July 1961, a fateful day, and a turning point when the tragedy of a serious car accident struck my otherwise normal life. I suffered extensive facial injuries and nearly lost the sight of both eyes. Before this accident, I never gave a thought to the deeper meaning of life. What was it all about? What was the purpose? I was floating on the surface of life, never knowing the treasures lying within.

At that point, out of the depth of my despair, my mind, my soul, was asking questions. I had no one I could ask who would be able to give me the answers. I found myself turning to God, crying out for understanding, guidance, and enlightenment, in my confused state of mind.

Strangely enough, or perhaps not strangely at all as I came to realise, answers began to come. One thing I learned is that every relationship is a two– way path, it can never be one way or we lose out. Our relationship with God is no different. I began at that point to communicate with God, my creator… I had no other option but to test the truth of the saying, "Ask and it shall be given to you, seek and ye shall find, knock and the door will open".

Having come from hospital and feeling at my lowest ebb, I cried out to God for help, for answers, and the words that filtered into my mind were "From Bitter Came Sweet" and "Now that you have lost the beauty without, seek the beauty within!" I was startled by this 'voice' or thought, which came to me. Thus began my spiritual journey and the extraordinary things that happened through which I came to realise that by far the most important and difficult journey to undertake is the journey within. However much we run around in circles, looking for peace and happiness in our material world, it can only be found buried within our own being. But before this happens we must find the answers to the most vital questions, "Who am I? Where did I come from, and where am I going from here?" Knowing the answers to these questions is the purpose of our life here.

My book is about this vital and illuminating journey, which has taken me many years to write. If it can help even one soul to find its way through this jungle of life, then my efforts will have been worthwhile.

PART ONE

Chapter 1

THE ACCIDENT

Nothing ever happens without a proper reason however accidental or mysterious it may appear.

Sathya Sai Baba

On July 11th 1961 I woke up in the morning. The sun was shining and everything looked bright and cheerful. It was a hot summer that year, the hottest for many years. I planned to go to London to pick up a friend who had arrived from abroad and take her shopping, dropping my two daughters at school on the way. Little did I know then that someone, somewhere, had another plan for me, and that 11th July, three days before my 33rd birthday, was to be a fateful day, a fate which was to turn my whole being and my life upside down and inside out, or rather outside in, as it turned out.

I picked up my friend at her hotel and we spent almost the entire day in and out of shops, buying the things on her long shopping list. I dropped her back at her hotel and was on my way to pick up my daughters from a friend in Harrow who had collected them from school. It was already 4 pm. By then I was quite exhausted and could not wait to get home and lie down and rest.

Whilst driving from Harrow to Neasden where we lived, I started to feel very sleepy. It was hot inside the car and the fact that my husband had insulated it the previous winter made it even hotter. I tried to open the window for a bit of fresh air, but the latch was stuck, the window just would not open.

As we arrived at the traffic lights, while waiting for the green signal, I could not stop my eyes closing and dozed off. I felt drained of energy, weak and faint, and must have been also somewhat dehydrated, since, during the day, we did not stop for a meal or even a drink as my friend wanted to complete her shopping before catching her plane the next day.

My twelve-year old daughter, Diana, was sitting beside me with her four-year old sister Poppy on her lap. Diana woke me up saying, "Mummy, it is the green light". I opened my eyes and drove on, but the same thing happened again at the next traffic light.

I was woken up again by my daughter and continued to drive home. I felt my eyelids getting heavier all the time and had to fight to keep my eyes open. At that point, as if I had an unconscious premonition, I asked my daughter Diana to put her sister Poppy on the back seat, but she insisted that her little sister remain seated on her lap. I again told her firmly to put her on the back seat and reluctantly she obeyed. I felt totally debilitated and could only think of one thing – I needed to lie down and close my eyes. However, that was not to be.

As we drove up a steep hill, I lost my struggle against sleep. Suddenly and tragically I was awakened by the impact of my head hitting the windscreen as my car hit another car, which had stopped by a nearby park gate. A couple apparently had just emerged from that car when I hit the door on the driver's side.

As I learned later, it was only a matter of a split second after the driver left his car that I hit the door out of which he had just stepped! That split second saved him from serious injury, or worse. I looked immediately to see if my daughters were all right and saw that Diana was already out of the car. She told me later on that when she realised I was going to hit the parked car, she had quickly opened the door and jumped out. In the back seat I saw that Poppy had fallen onto the floor. They were both crying. I thanked God I had insisted on her being moved to the back seat. Had she still been sitting on her sister's lap, they would both have been trapped in the car and seriously injured. There were, unfortunately, no seat belts in cars in 1961.

People gathered seemingly from nowhere. They must have heard the noise of the impact and came out to see what had happened. I was taken out of the car and seated on the pavement by the park gate. I heard my daughters crying but was assured that they had not been hurt. I was greatly relieved and thankful that no one else had been injured. Someone asked for my husband's telephone number and went to call him.

A short distance from the park was a local private hospital. A man in the crowd said he would go and ask for assistance from the hospital. While waiting for help to come, I ran my fingers across my face to feel what my injuries were as I was not feeling any pain. I felt my face. It was wet and sticky. I knew that it was blood. I put my hands over my right eye and to my horror it felt hollow, I could not feel the eyeball. I knew immediately that I had lost my right eye. I cannot begin to describe my utter shock, disbelief and horror at what had happened to me. In one split second everything had changed. My life would never be the same again. I was never going to be the same again. Was it a bad dream? I wished it had been, but the reality of it, the devastating reality, began to sink in. I said over and over again to the people who were standing near me: "I have lost my eye, I have lost my eye". I heard the people say that an ambulance would soon arrive.

Meanwhile the news from the nearby hospital was unexpected and unthinkable. They did not want to get involved. They did not even send a nurse or a doctor to give first aid, knowing that there had been two young children involved in the accident, one of whom, Diana, was bleeding from cuts caused by flying glass from the windscreen. Their help could have been crucial in saving a life if there had been profuse bleeding.

After twenty minutes an ambulance arrived. I was numb with shock to such a degree that notwithstanding the horrific injuries, I felt no physical pain. How strange that, in spite of extensive injuries and the traumatic experience, I felt totally calm.

The ambulance arrived at Neasden Eye Hospital. As I was wheeled in, a taxi stopped by the entrance and out came a gentleman whom I was later told was one of the top eye surgeons in the country. He was just going to stop for a minute to give instructions about one of his patients as he was on his way to the airport to attend an important conference in Scotland where he was to be the main speaker. As fate would have it, he happened to enter the hospital at the same time as I was being wheeled in, actually walking alongside my stretcher.

One of the hospital staff approached him immediately, saying that I was a serious case and there was no one else with his experience to deal with it. The taxi was sent away and Mr. Jackson, having no choice, agreed to perform the operation and was at once handed the 'white coat'. He entered the operating theatre, visibly annoyed that he would have to miss his important conference.

The staff later told me how fortunate I was to have had such an eminent eye surgeon to perform the operation. The incredible timing was too extraordinary to be a 'coincidence'. Had he not been there, there is no doubt that I would have lost the sight of both my eyes and my face would also have been permanently disfigured.

After the operation I was told that due to the fact that the eye was cut through the middle of the pupil and iris, the eye had sunk into its socket. It had, therefore, to be pulled out, stitched together and re-positioned in the socket. It was a delicate and difficult operation and with very little chance of success. It took over four hours to perform the eye operation and to deal with the extensive facial injuries, which had to be attended to immediately to prevent permanent scarring and disfigurement. Afterward Mr. Jackson explained that the cuts on my face were like a jigsaw puzzle, which had to be put together. This had involved 100 stitches! He had done all he could and it was now, in his words, "in God's hands".

Again I realised how very 'lucky' I was to have had this most eminent surgeon to perform such an intricate operation! Was it 'coincidence that Mr. Jackson had arrived at the very moment that I was wheeled in? One might think so when it happens, but, since my accident, too many 'coincidences' have occurred and always at a crucial moment when timing was of the essence. Through these experiences I came to the conclusion that there must be a power or something beyond our understanding that comes to our aid in times of need. Perhaps these experiences are sent to awaken us to this realisation.

Following the operation, I was put into a ward with one other patient who happened to be the nurse for whom the surgeon had come to give instructions as to her treatment during his absence in Scotland. The room was fairly large with a window opposite the entrance. The nurse's bed was by the window and mine was against the wall near the door. There was a screen in the middle of the room separating us. We were the only patients in this large ward.

With a heavily bandaged eye, I was lying on the bed numb with shock. Would I wake up from this nightmare and find out that it was just a bad dream? How I wished it were, but no, to my horror, I realised that this was 'real'. I now had to learn to live with a new 'me'. Nothing would ever be the same again. I was shattered, crushed, disfigured and bewildered. I could not think anymore. I only knew that I did not want to carry on living. I wished I was dead.

While touching the bandage over my eye, I ran my hand over my face and felt stitches everywhere. How could I face myself and live like this with such disfigurement? I just did not want to carry on living, yet I had to think of my two little girls whom I could not leave without a mother. What could I possibly do, how would I cope? All sorts of thoughts raced through my mind, until I could bear no more. Suddenly I just had to let go. I gave up and sank into a state of quiet resignation, my mind quite numb, and beyond thought.

Again, was it 'coincidence' that on the day of the accident, my husband's secretary did not arrive at work as she fell ill and a temporary secretary came to replace her? She was in his office when my husband received the telephone call informing him of my accident and heard what had happened. Seeing my husband in a state of shock, she told him that she knew a very good spiritual healer whom she was sure could help me. She said that she would arrange an appointment for me to see this healer when I came out of hospital, if I would be willing. She told my husband that she would like to visit me in hospital and tell me about it. When my husband came to see me he mentioned it to me and I agreed, as any help, from whatever source, which could offer even a glimmer of hope, was worth trying.

The next day, at visiting time, my husband's new secretary walked into my room, introducing herself as Tania. She was a pretty girl, brunette, in her middle twenties and seemed sincere. She told me of the wonderful healing the elderly Egyptian man had been giving her for a serious eye condition, which doctors could not help her with, and said that there now was a remarkable improvement. She said she would ask him to see me when I came out of hospital if I wished. I said that I would be very willing to go anywhere, try anything, and see anyone who could help me.

Again, 'strange' as it may seem, the day after Tania's visit, something extraordinary happened to me. It was mid-afternoon. I was lying in a state of complete numbness, not caring anymore whether I lived or died, a total letting-go of body and mind. I could think of nothing. I was not able and did not want to think. I had lost all sense of time and must have been half-dozing, half-awake, when suddenly I saw an enormous circle of intense, bright, white light on the side of my injured right eye. I cannot describe the brightness; the light was so strong that I instinctively turned my face towards it, thinking that it was night time since my eyes were closed, and that the nurse had come in with a torch to check if I was all right.

On opening my left eye, I noticed that it was three o'clock in the afternoon, there was no one in the room and all was quiet. I realised that this intense light was not coming from the window. I closed my eye again, thinking that maybe it was my imagination, but on closing my eye again, there came again this flood of light forming a circle around my injured eye.

Three times this happened whenever I opened and then closed my eye. After the third time it was no longer there. My mind started racing with thoughts, I was bewildered by this experience, but enjoyed the comfort it gave me. I wondered whether it could have any meaning. Was it a sign that I would not lose my eye after all and that somehow I would be all right in the end? I was not sure, but felt in my inner being that it was a sign bringing a flicker of hope into my sinking heart, even though the surgeon had prepared my husband for the likelihood that the odds were against my eye being saved. My wish to die was giving way to a faint hope. Could a miracle really happen to me? Was the bright light indeed a spiritual experience or a divine sign?

I remained in hospital for ten days. I arrived home a different person from the one who had left on the morning of 11th July 1961. I was totally changed, physically, mentally, and emotionally. I had to face up to the awful reality of my 'new look' – there wasn't a place on my face without stitches. My eye did not resemble an eye – there was no iris or pupil to be seen, just a red blob of blood. I cannot describe the sickly feeling at seeing such a disfigurement. How could I live with myself? The image, which confronted me, was not I but a stranger, yet I knew that, hard as it might be to accept, the reality stared back at me. There was no escape, that was the 'new' me. How would I cope? I did not know, only God knew, and it was to Him I would turn at my lowest ebb. Praying to Him in the depth of my despair, He did not ignore my plight, as subsequent events would reveal.

Next morning, after my first night at home, I put on a pair of dark glasses to hide the terrible sight of my eye, and never took them off until I went to bed at night. I could not bear to see the sunlight. I could not even listen to music. It reminded me of the times when I was carefree, looked good, and enjoyed the sunny days and favourite tunes. Looking at myself now horrified me and I soon learned to do my hair and put on my make-up without ever looking in the mirror.

When I was discharged from hospital, the doctor had instructed me to have a check-up at the Out-patients Department every day as he feared that the infection, which I still had in the injured eye, would spread to my good eye and put it at risk. He kept a very close check on this. I felt that the eye was not yet secure in its socket, which made me walk as if on egg-shells, fearing to bend or do any sudden movements which might jeopardise the eye. Each hospital visit was a nightmare. Fearful thoughts assailed me. Had the infection spread? Would they have to remove the eye today?

Meanwhile, Tania, (my husband's new secretary) had arranged the appointment with Mr. St. George, the healer. The appointment was for 7 p.m. that day. My husband and I left home at Neasden and drove to Kensington, somewhere behind Barkers Department Store.

We rang the bell and an elderly man, short in stature, oriental looking, opened the door. With a reassuring smile he showed us into his study, which was in the basement of the house. The room looked more like a library. Every wall was covered with books. The curtains were drawn and the room, in semi-darkness, lit only by a dim light. The atmosphere was quiet and peaceful. He asked us to sit down near him by his desk. He reached out his hands and asked us to link our hands with his in a circle. He then said a prayer, telling us to close our eyes and relax.

All of a sudden, I started to experience a current-like sensation, with heat moving up my right hand and arm reaching my right eye! The eyeball started to vibrate in its socket, first gently and then the vibration became stronger and stronger. I started to worry as the eye was so fragile after the operation and felt insecure in its socket. I was concerned that this strong, moving and shaking sensation, which I was experiencing, might harm it. I felt as if the eyeball was going to pop out any minute.

Panicking, I interrupted the silence and told Mr. St. George what I was experiencing. He told me, in his quiet reassuring voice, not to worry, but asked me to keep my eyes closed, which I did instinctively anyway.

We sat holding hands for about twenty minutes. The healer then ended with a prayer and said that I could come for healing once more if I wished. I said that I would like to come again and he made an appointment for the following week. All the way home in the car my eyeball was still vibrating, shaking in its socket. However, it gradually slowed down, and, by the time I went to bed, it vibrated only faintly. I had a sound and peaceful sleep that night for the first time without taking any sleeping pills.

In the morning, on waking up, I wanted to look in the mirror to see how the vibrations had affected my eye. I had to muster quite a bit of courage to do this. I walked towards the bathroom mirror shaking with fear at what I might see. I glanced at my eye and, to my amazement, I saw that the inside corner of the eye showed a little bit of white where before the whole eyeball was a red blob due to the infection. I realised this meant that the infection was beginning to show signs of clearing up. This was most encouraging. Perhaps my injured eye could be saved after all. I breathed a deep sigh of relief. I began to have hope, and felt that the healing of the previous evening was the miracle for which I had been praying.

That morning I was due for my daily outpatient visit at the hospital. On arrival I was shown into Mr. Jackson's room and sat down trembling with fear about Mr. Jackson's prognosis. I knew that he did not have much hope that my eye could be saved. As he came over to examine my eye, I was anxiously watching the expression on his face. As he looked into the eye with his instrument for the second time, I could see his look of incredulity. Looking again straight at me, he said, "What have you done? I can't understand what has happened since yesterday".

I was gripped with terror at what he might tell me. Perhaps he would now say that my eye would have to be removed. I did not dare tell him about the spiritual healing I had received and the vibration of the eyeball I had experienced, thinking that perhaps this had caused some damage and was the reason he was reacting in this way. My heart sank, thinking again, "that's it! Now he will tell me that I will have to go back into hospital to have the eye removed." Without saying a word to me, he left the room, leaving me sitting on my own, dreading what I was going to hear when he returned.

He came back with two colleagues. Saying nothing to me, they each in turn examined my eye with a light and looked at each other puzzled. They were obviously bewildered at what they were seeing. I felt it was the positive change overnight which astonished them and I hoped that I was right in this assumption.

Mr. Jackson turned to me saying, "You are a bloody lucky girl", (these were the words he used), "The infection seems to be moving away and if it continues to improve, you will not lose your eye!" My whole body, which was tense with fear and anxiety, sank with relief. Going home I thanked God for His mercy and grace, thinking about the bright light I had seen whilst in hospital, and felt an inner conviction that it was indeed a divine sign, a blessing.

However, a long period of darkness within and darkness without followed. Little did I know that out of this darkness would sprout the spiritual seed buried deep inside me? Out of the turmoil and confusion, came knowledge, understanding and light. I learned that what happens to us is meant for our highest good, even if we do not see it that way or understand God's plan for us. However, this understanding or realisation did not happen overnight.

My struggle had only just begun. As each morning dawned, after a night of sleep and forgetfulness, I was constantly reminded of the reality of my terrible injuries. An intense fear would grip my heart, so much so that at times I could scarcely breathe. How could I come to terms with this drastic change in my appearance?

The following week my husband took me once more to see the healer to whom I shall always feel such a debt of gratitude. He had put me on the road to recovery, although it was to be a slow and painful upward climb. In spite of moments of despair, I was determined to hang on. Hope had been kindled in my heart through the first two signs, the experience of the light in the hospital and the miracle healing, which came in its wake.

Meanwhile, home had become my prison, as I could not face the outside world. I did not want to meet people. I could not bear to see the sunlight. I could not listen to music. All this was associated with my former carefree self, my life before the accident.

I knew I needed help, but who could help me? Where should I go to find it? In the meantime I went through patches of black moods created by my fearful thoughts. The idea of suicide was entering my mind, however much I tried to push it away. But how on earth could I do that? The thought frightened me, as I felt that at some point I might give way to this unthinkable impulse. It seemed to me that it was a matter of 'when' and not 'if'; so dark was the outlook.

I visualised ending my life, but the thought of my two little girls being left without a mother to care for them was unthinkable. I made up my mind there and then that I would fight on for as long as needed to overcome this tragedy and learn to live my life and smile again, if only for their sake. I owed it to my children. They were my responsibility and I had no right to run away or give up.

From this time on, the road was long and painful, as all kinds of thoughts, one minute positive, the next minute negative, played havoc with my already troubled mind. At times I feared for my sanity. I went to the doctor. All he could do was to prescribe tranquillisers but this did not help. They left me even more depressed. I stopped taking the pills. I resolved yet again that, once and for all, I had to gather the scattered, shattered pieces of my life and put them together, but how was I going to do it? Where would I get the strength and the help? If only I could talk to someone, an old wise man who could explain why this had happened to me, someone who could reassure and enlighten me as to what this life was all about.

Out of my utter hopelessness, I one day fell on to my knees in desperate supplication and prayer for help. The words I heard myself say astonished me. I was crying out, "God, I love you; God, I love you", repeating it several times. "Please help me, show me what to do, how to live with myself, please show me the way – your way....". Tears poured down my face. I was still kneeling when the following words filtered into my mind: "From Bitter Came Sweet"!

I was bewildered by these words. I reflected on them, remembering that similar words came from the Old Testament story of Samson and Delilah. At first, I could not understand why such words should come to my mind. Perhaps the message meant that, although I was going through a bitter experience, things would turn sweet in the end, but it was hard to imagine how, in my condition. I told myself that I had to hold on and see if, what I had received as a guiding thought would prove to be true.

It was in the afternoons when I would be resting in my room with curtains drawn, that I would receive these guiding thoughts and revelations. As I lay thinking of the bleak future with a sinking heart, once again the following thought filtered into my mind. It was strong and clear - "Now that you have lost the beauty without, seek the beauty within"!

As I lay, reflecting on this, I realised that I had been living very much on the surface of life, relying on the good looks I was born with. This had somewhat compensated for the traumatic childhood and lack of love and understanding I experienced before my arranged marriage at the age of 17. However, now even this had been taken from me. I now had to work on myself, to seek and develop the beauty within. This was the profound message I had received.

Although puzzled, I knew in my heart that a new path lay ahead – to discover another me. The time had arrived for a change in attitude, a change in my whole outlook on life, but how was it to come about and what should I do? This was not yet clear to me. I awaited further guidance.

Lying on my bed at noon one day, feeling very low, still unable to come to terms with what had happened, my mind was once again going through negative and destructive thoughts. The contemplation of suicide was still nagging and worrying me. I was afraid that I might give in to this impulse in a moment of weakness, turning on the gas or harming myself in some way. As always at this crucial moment, my thoughts turned to my two young daughters at school who would be waiting to be collected at 4 p.m. I could not bear the thought of leaving my children without a mother. Under a strong impulse I rushed downstairs, threw a coat over my shoulders and closed the door behind me. Walking down my street, I did not know where I was heading. I just felt that I was safer outside the house. Somehow I found myself walking towards Gladstone Park, which was close to our house. I entered the park with tears rolling down my face. There was no one else to be seen, just the trees silently dripping rain over me as if crying with me.

I was shivering from cold and depression. I found myself heading towards the library at the other end of the park, even if only to get out of the rain and into a warm place. As I entered the library I did not know what to do. I certainly could not think of reading a book, my mind was not up to it, but somehow I felt my hand reach up and take down a book at random from the nearest shelf. The title of the book was *'The Secret Path'* by Dr. Paul Brunton. I opened the cover and began to read. His words of wisdom spoke directly to me.

At home, I continued to read it with intense interest. Every line was like balm to an open wound. I began to understand that we are, in 'essence', not just a physical being as I had always thought. I realised that our true self was of the 'spirit'. I was drawn to find out more about Dr. Brunton's experiences in the spiritual dimension and his philosophy. Somehow his words rang a bell within my inner being and began to give me the strength I so much needed. I even began to see a purpose in what had happened to me, strange, as it seemed. I felt strength and hope enter my being. I had to find out more, much more. This book proved to be my guiding light, the answers to so many of the questions to my bewildered mind. I hoped I had begun my journey of self-discovery.

I began to read more of Paul Brunton's books. I found them gripping, illuminating and uplifting. Here was what I so much needed, here was the 'wise man' I had prayed for, talking to me through the pages of his books. This led me on to read books written by those who had overcome tragedies in their own lives, as well as other spiritual literature.

At the time of my accident in 1961, the subjects of Yoga, meditation or spiritual enquiries, were much frowned upon, and people were inclined to regard those interested in such subjects as cranks. But to me, however, all this new knowledge gripped my inner being with a feeling of truth.

Who was this man, Dr. Paul Brunton? He was born in London in 1898. Early in life he became interested in comparative religion and philosophy. He travelled extensively in the Orient, investigating ideas and practices of yogis, mystics and holy men. He lived among them in their monasteries, retreats and hermitages.

He dedicated his book 'The Wisdom of the Overself', *"To those sincere pioneers of a nobler epoch whose deep need and silent thoughts called forth this book".* How strange, but perhaps not so strange, that Paul Brunton, 'the old and wise man', was to lead me on my inner search and discovery about our true reality! He lit the light in my darkened soul.

In his book 'The Secret Path', he wrote:

> *"He who would heal the wounded souls of others must have first suffered himself. He only has a right to give words of hope and to pronounce phrases of faith unto men, who has himself walked wearily through the night of despair and has come at last out of the shadow of deep melancholy. Because he too has lain awake at night sweating in stark agony and fearing the horror of another hopeless day....".*

How appropriate and prophetic Dr. Brunton's words turned out to be in my life after the accident.

His words inspired me deeply. They lifted the materialistic veil, which had blinded me for half my life, and set me on the inner quest.

In his book, 'A Message from Arunachala, Paul Brunton states:

"After all, the best aristocracy is that of the soul. A man is great, not because he was born into an exalted rank, but because he was born with an exalted soul".

"If only people would let go of everything for a few minutes every day, dropping all tension, relaxing every muscle of the body, reposing the mind and slowing the breath, they might begin to provide the requisite conditions whereby the Overself could make its serenity felt throughout their lives. Thus they would daily learn to withdraw quietly into its peace. Nor would their activities really suffer, even though a little time had been stolen from them. For life would become more balanced, duties would be carried out in a calmer and more collected manner, each crisis or emergency would find them both ready and steady, free from panic".

"Love is the most powerful force in the universe. That is why the Supreme Being must ultimately conquer the world. For He loves His creatures so much that they will all yield themselves completely to Him one day".

These were the words that set me on the path of self-discovery; words that removed the dark thoughts from my mind and gave me renewed hope in life.

Chapter 2

SPIRITUAL EXPERIENCES

Do not flinch in the face of grief.
Welcome the test because thereafter you are awarded the certificate. It is to measure your progress that tests are imposed.

Sathya Sai Baba

As I lay in bed one afternoon, conscious of my surroundings but in a state of passive submission, my eyes closed, I suddenly saw a vision as though a television screen had opened in the centre of my forehead between my eyebrows. I beheld the face of an elderly Greek or Russian Orthodox Priest, which I recognised by his headdress. I saw him distinctly and vividly as if he was there in the flesh in front of me. He had a serene countenance and a beard, which covered most of his face, and half his chest, on which hung a large ornate crucifix on a heavy chain. He appeared in close view only down to his waist.

He said nothing, but looked straight at me. I instinctively opened my eyes but he was not in the room. I closed my eyes and saw him inwardly only, once more after which he was gone. I was extremely puzzled by it. From what I learned later, I understood that we could receive such visions from the opening of the 'third eye', which is between the two eyebrows in the middle of the forehead.

What did this vision mean? Why a religious Christian figure when I am of the Jewish faith? I had no answer but understanding of its significance came years later. At the precise moment I felt strongly that it came to give me hope and courage to face up to what I had to go through. I began to have the feeling that I was not alone. Perhaps it came to show me that there is something beyond the physical. I was waiting for further developments. Meanwhile, I began to look forward with hope and anticipation.

Strange things were happening to me almost daily during this period. Most of them I jotted down on paper at the time lest I should forget. While taking my usual rest in the afternoon, with curtains drawn, my soul, my thoughts were in the darkness of my melancholy. I lay under the quilt cover. As I turned over to my left side I felt a chill on my exposed back. Before I could move my hand to cover myself, I suddenly felt the quilt being slowly pulled over me, so gently that I was mystified by it. Tears came to my eyes, realising that someone gentle and loving was present although invisible to me, one who yet wanted to comfort me. With this encouragement and guidance I could now somehow cope a little better each day. I prayed ceaselessly to God to give me strength to cope. These strange happenings gave me the strength I needed.

On another occasion, lying under the quilt cover, I suddenly felt a gentle pressure on my feet. At first I thought that the cat might have slipped into my bedroom and jumped onto the bed, although I remembered closing the door of my bedroom. I opened my eyes but there was no cat. Instead, I felt the presence of a loving being who gave me a feeling of peace, and to whom I sent words of gratitude. I had no doubt these happenings were meant to give me a message of hope, that I was going to be all right, and that I should hold on. The depression and sense of hopelessness did not disappear overnight, but I realised I had to work at it with all my courage and strength. No psychiatrist or 'angel' could just appear and wipe away my problem with a magic wand. It was up to me alone to deal with it.

I made up my mind that I would start to get acquainted with my Inner Self, to bring out the 'beauty from within' as the voice had told me. There was no other path that I could take. With the gentle encouragement that I was blessed to receive, I vowed that no matter how long it would take, I was going to transform myself, and win the battle with my lower self. I would truly become stronger, more positive and cheerful, to be able to cope better with life for the sake of my family. I was determined to forget myself and live to serve. I would find happiness in the happiness of others. I surrendered my whole being to that purpose, to let God use me to do whatever He willed. That way was surely better than ending my life out of selfishness and self-pity.

I prayed for strength and courage to cope for just one day at a time – I could not think as far as the next week or even the next day. Through my prayers, my faith was strengthened daily by the inspiration and experiences I was receiving, and the help and guidance, which, whenever I needed them, were somehow always forthcoming.

One afternoon as I was leaving the house, my neighbour approached me. She said a few words of sympathy regarding my accident and asked me if I would be interested in seeing a healer. She related to me the case of her niece who had one leg two inches shorter than the other and had to wear a special shoe. Being a young girl, she was self-conscious and had a complex about her disability. She would not go out and mix with young people of her own age. Her mother took her to a spiritual healer, and, after some healing; quite incredibly, the shorter leg grew to the same length as the other leg. She could then wear ordinary shoes and feel normal. She started going out, had a boy friend, and began leading a life like any other girl of her age, something she thought she would never be able to do.

I listened to this case with almost disbelief, but knew my neighbour was telling the truth. I asked her how I could contact a healer, as I would be prepared to go anywhere if there was any hope. She gave me a copy of the 'Psychic News'. I looked through the columns of healers and picked out a few names to telephone. I chose two names and started going once a week to each of them. I found both the healers to be very compassionate, warm and caring people who, unlike doctors, had more time for you as a person. My children were very young, my husband was involved in business, and I did not want to add to his burden. I fought my mental and emotional battles alone. I had great admiration for the way these healers worked, totally selflessly, caring sincerely about people and their problems.

After receiving healing from these two healers, I happened to read an article in 'Psychic News' about Mr. George Jessup, a healer as well as a medium who lived near Victoria Station. I felt an impulse to telephone him and booked an appointment. When I arrived and entered his flat, I felt vibrations of great peace and spirituality. George was an elderly man of about seventy years, white-haired, quiet, gentle and reassuring. He and his wife received me with great warmth and made me feel very welcome and at home.

I continued to go to him for healing regularly for about a year. Every time after the healing session we had tea together and George and his wife René used to enlighten me about the Spiritual Realms of which I had little or no knowledge at the time. I learnt a great deal from these discussions, which helped to lift my depression. I began to see things more in perspective. On one occasion George told me that one day I too would be a healer and that, when he passed on, he would help me from the 'other side' in my healing.

I looked at him in utter surprise and disbelief. He then took a piece of paper and wrote the following prayer for me, the words of which proved to be prophetic: -

Help me to live from day to day
In such a self-forgetful way –
That even when I kneel to pray
My prayers will be for others

Help me in the work I do
To always be sincere and true –
And know – that all I'd do for you
Must need's be done for others

Let self be crucified and slain
And buried deep –
And efforts be to rise again –
Unless it be for others

Others, Lord yes, others –
Let this my motto be,
Help me to live for others
That I may live like Thee.

One afternoon, whilst resting at home when these visions or revelations had a habit of occurring, I saw the Bible opened to my inner gaze. I was reading a beautiful passage from it, which I cannot remember ever having previously read or learnt. I opened my eyes, to see only my bedroom furniture. I realised yet again that I was 'seeing' these visions not with my physical eyes but with my inner eye, or the third eye as I had come to understand it. I regretted not having a pen and paper by my bedside to write down what I had just 'read'. Tears of joy always filled my eyes after these experiences.

Looking at my watch I saw it was time to get up and collect the girls from school. I thought "I will remember and write it down later", but on returning to the house with my girls, listening to them chatting away and answering their questions, I could no longer remember what I had read in my vision. It was as if a veil or a door had closed in my mind and I could no longer recall it. I saw the Bible opened to my inner gaze many more times over the years, but was unable to recall what was written on the page as had happened on the first occasion. I just knew it was the Bible and recognised the style of writing as the Holy Scriptures. It was the Old Testament I saw. It had, I felt, a spiritual significance for me. I was uplifted and grateful for it.

I still confined myself to home, and avoided going out to meet people, unless absolutely necessary. Meanwhile I wanted to occupy my time at home with something positive. Again guidance was at hand. As I prayed, an answer was not long in coming. I picked up a paper and read an advertisement about a correspondence course in Psychology. That was just what I needed. I immediately enrolled and started on the course, it gave me a sense of achievement when I received the examination papers marked with a high pass grade. The subject filled me with a little more self-understanding and helped me to look at things more positively. The course took about a year and gave me a sense of achievement. A year had passed and I was still alive! However, I had not yet emerged fully from my sense of despair and desolation, although I was coping better, and still praying for guidance and direction.

My husband's business was thriving, which enabled us to live a comfortable, indeed affluent life, but this did not lessen my spiritual yearnings. I realised that no amount of money, material possessions or social standing could satisfy the longing of my soul.

I had begun attending occasionally the Spiritualist Association of Great Britain in Belgrave Square, sometimes to see mediums or attend lectures. One day, looking at the bookstall in the hall, my eyes were drawn to a picture on the cover of a book entitled *'Autobiography of a Yogi'*, written by Paramahansa Yogananda. Something about the serene and peaceful look on the face of this Indian Yogi impelled me to buy the book. I started reading it immediately. Each line in this book vibrated with Divine Love and Wisdom.The words had great spiritual power to which I was drawn. Here was a practical philosophy, not a religion, which I wanted to follow. Once again Divine Guidance was at work!

Yogananda was the first Yogi to come to the West to teach yoga and meditation. He went to the United States of America in 1920 and later on founded the Self-Realisation Fellowship Organisation in Los Angeles, lecturing on the technique of meditation. I lost no time and enrolled for the lessons, which turned out to be a seven-year correspondence course!

Through the lessons and answering questions set at the end of each week, the student gradually progressed along the path of spiritual enlightenment and realisation. This gave me greater strength and sense of purpose, a positive path to follow.

After a year of studying, I was initiated into the Kriya Yoga technique. My feet were put onto the first rung of the spiritual ladder. I knew I was on the right path. It reminded me of the saying from the Bible, "Ask and it will be given unto you, seek and ye shall find, knock and the door shall be opened unto you". I was testing this saying. It has never failed me.

I used to practice yoga and meditation daily in my little dressing room. On one occasion when I was deep in meditation I was suddenly aware of a strong aroma of incense, which gave me a feeling of Divine Love and Peace. I could not control my tears as I gave thanks for this experience. I felt that it was once again a sign that I was not alone.

On another occasion, while meditating, a heavenly fragrance of freesias filled my small meditation room – it was so moving and uplifting. I knew it was not from my garden as I had no freesias nor did I have any in the house. Where could it have suddenly come from? I had no doubt that it was to draw my attention to a higher realm – another dimension. These were the thoughts on which I began to ponder.

Once, deep in meditation, I suddenly felt myself lifted from my chair! I was, in fact, being levitated a few inches above the chair I had been sitting on. I felt very light. I was floating and feeling as if I came out of my body. It must have been an out-of-body experience, which, frankly, gave me such a fright that I willed myself back into my body and onto the chair. Since then I have taken great care not to let it happen again.

One afternoon, while resting, I found myself between two states of consciousness, not asleep yet not fully awake, in a state of 'limbo'. Suddenly, I heard my name being called clearly; "Ruth, Ruth!" The sound came from behind me above my head. I turned instinctively towards the direction of the voice. There was no one there. I knew I would not be able to see anything with my physical eyes, so I turned my thoughts inward and asked a question. My mental question was, "Why has this accident happened to me in such a terrible way?" The answer came immediately, as a thought in my mind, that it was because I was living dangerously (perhaps referring to my fast driving). Also, I knew, in respect to my life in general, that I would rush into going places or doing things without, thinking as to whether this was important or necessary at all – it seemed that I was unconsciously running away from something – perhaps from myself.

There was a constant restlessness within me. I could never just sit quietly and relax. This accident had come to awaken me to a deeper meaning and purpose of life. I therefore knew what this message meant and accepted the higher wisdom that it had come to teach me, though in such a painful way.

At times, at my lowest, I would cross roads without looking left or right, hoping that a car would put an end to my misery, but somehow they would stop just an inch from me. It seemed that I was meant to bear my cross and find the spiritual path, which would help me cope. Only by accepting what I could not change and surrendering to the Higher Intelligence, or God, could I find peace and contentment.

I now knew without a doubt that I was not alone. I was receiving help and guidance. I realised how fortunate I was. I had to make every effort to be worthy of it, by self-improvement, looking within myself, - and changing whatever traits or weaknesses I knew needed change, difficult though it might be. Even if it took the rest of my life to achieve, that was now my goal. However many times I might fail, I would try and try again. I would never give up that goal – this I promised myself.

On another occasion, half asleep, half awake, totally relaxed, an image appeared to me. I saw a beautiful meadow, quite indescribable in words. Its vivid colours of green grass and multi-coloured flowers made our earthly grass and flowers seem faded by comparison. It was breathtakingly beautiful and tranquil, and made me wonder whether I was seeing a glimpse of heaven or the spirit world. This experience was not to repeat itself, but I was left with a feeling of peace, love and gratitude.

Once, when in a state of deep depression, feeling that my life was not worth living any more, a thought came to me that I could perhaps do something for people who were in need. Suddenly an idea came to my mind to go to the nearest hospital to visit someone who was alone and had no visitors, take him/her some fruit or flowers just to cheer him/her up. At least I would be of some use to others.

I bought a bunch of grapes, and went to the nearest hospital, which happened to be St. Andrews. I explained to the Sister-in-charge why I was there and she showed me to the bed of an elderly man. As I was standing near her, she spoke to the patient telling him that I had come to visit someone who did not have any visitors and would he mind if I had a few words with him. He looked surprised but agreed, so I pulled up a chair and sat near him giving him the bunch of grapes. I stayed a short while chatting to him, wished him well, and returned home.

Walking back, I remembered how touched the elderly man was by my unexpected visit. It made me feel I had done something worthwhile instead of thinking only of my own misery. I continued to visit lonely patients in the hospital, taking fruit or flowers. Doing this gave me a sense of purpose, a feeling of worthiness.

Often dreams come to give a message, or to reveal something, which is going to happen. The following dream was one with a significant message for me. On 11th March 1976, I made a note of the following dream, which, on waking, left a deep impression on me. A vast ocean that stretched beyond and into infinity surrounded me. There was nothing around as far as the eye could see; only the sea, and I was in the middle of it. I did not know how I would find my way towards the shore, as I could not see where the shore might be. It seemed impossible. I feared I would just drown. I would never have the strength to swim in that vast ocean to find land, let alone know the direction in which to aim. I tried to swim, but felt unable to advance even an inch as the strength of the current was pushing me back.

Just as I felt that there was no hope and I was about to give up through sheer exhaustion, I saw a wooden barrier appear like a fence in a straight line in the middle of the ocean close to me. I was able to grab hold of the fence, which gave me a little respite to get my breath back. The fence seemed to extend in a straight line as far as the horizon, so I felt that just by pulling myself along it bit by bit, I would eventually reach the shore. Indeed, as I advanced slowly holding on to this support, I knew that at least it would stop me from drowning.

I woke up from this vivid dream with a strong feeling that it contained an important message for me. I began to see clearly what it was meant to convey; that the tragedy of my car accident which had left me so vulnerable and insecure, drowning me in such sorrow that I could not see the light at the end of the dark tunnel – this was the strong current of the ocean preventing me from going forward. The fence represented God whom I had to hold on to for dear life, as only with His support would I be led across the turbulent sea of life to safety and security. How prophetic this dream turned out to be!

Indeed, as the dream of the ocean taught me, I have, through the years of upheavals, tragedies and turbulence, held on tenaciously to the 'fence', keeping God's name constantly in my mind, and on my lips. It has, by His Grace, seen me through it all to the safety of the shore of light, peace, and contentment.

Referring back to the time of my accident when my mind was confused and I was still in shock, struggling to make sense of it all, I happened to look amongst some old photographs. One that turned out to be very significant came to my hand. It was a picture taken in Beirut in Lebanon when I was twelve years old.

My mind went back to my early years in Israel, where we lived. During the summer holidays my mother used to take my younger sister and myself to Beirut to visit my aunt and cousins who lived there. A picture was taken of my cousin Helen, my sister Miki and myself standing side by side. Looking at it, I noticed that there was a cross over my head in the photograph! It was as if the cross-had been planted right over the middle of my head, dead centre. I was amazed and looked at the photograph for a few moments wondering why I had never noticed this before.

It must have been there all the time, yet had only come into my awareness now! It made me think of it's meaning, in view of all that had happened to me. The cross could have appeared anywhere in the photograph, yet it was over my head. I felt in my heart that this was no coincidence but that there was a message in it for me. The picture had a double significance, symbolising the spiritual path, which I was to take, and the 'crosses' I had to bear from childhood to adulthood.

My accident was the means by which I was to be turned from the outer material world, to the inner world of Spirituality. I felt it was a call to serve God. At that time I did not know how. I felt sure time would tell. As years rolled on, the pattern of this path gradually unfolded. It led to my becoming a spiritual healer years later, and to other discoveries of the world of the spirit.

Once again, while lying half awake, half asleep, I had a vision of Jesus nailed to the Cross vividly appear in front of me. His face showed his great suffering and my heart went out to him in his agony. I felt my hand immediately move forward as I wanted to lift him up, to ease his pain. On opening my eyes, the vision vanished. My face was wet with tears. I was overwhelmed with feelings of love and deep compassion that stayed with me for a long while. I could not understand the significance of this at the time. I did later.

Another experience, which I noted at the time, occurred when I awoke on 24th October 1986 between 3-4 a.m. Following a hurtful experience of a personal nature, I went to sleep praying for health, strength and calmness, and also wisdom to cope with the problem. Suddenly I heard a voice in my right ear, as if someone was whispering into it. It was a woman's voice and although I cannot remember what she said, I asked her in thought "Who are you?" I got the answer 'Judy' or 'Judith'. I knew no one by this name. I then felt a hand touching my face gently. I put my hand on top of that hand and felt the lovely soft smooth skin of that person. I wanted to pull her fingers to my lips to kiss them, but 'Judy' pulled them away. I felt her face close to my right cheek so I touched her cheek that felt as warm and soft as a baby's face.

I woke up. As had happened before, when I was in great need of reassurance and help, this never failed to come. I understood it to be a sign that I was not alone. I am loved, cared about and protected by this invisible but tangible spirit who comes as a reassuring sign to comfort me and give me strength to continue in the knowledge that I am not abandoned. Help is always at hand at the crucial moment.

I so much wanted to have this soft and gentle person to stay with me forever, as it gave me such comfort, but the thought came into my mind as an answer: "We cannot stay and interfere in your life. It is important you grow spiritually through all the experiences. If we did, you would not grow and develop but depend on others". How well I understood that. This experience, as with others, made me shed tears of joy. My heart was filled with humility and gratitude for such a privilege. I thank 'Judy' for the help and the unexpected comfort and kindness she gave me.

Chapter 3

HEALING

"Faith in God is the tonic that man needs to get back health and happiness"

Sathya Sai Baba

As time passed, I began to feel a great desire to alleviate the suffering of those I saw who were in pain or disabled. I felt an overwhelming sense of compassion. I wanted to lay my hands on people, to bring comfort, hope and upliftment, to let them know that someone cared and wished them well. I sent out a prayer as I passed them by. I do not know why I did this, as my own heart was still full of sadness.

It was difficult to feel inner joy or peace. However, I put my own misery to one side and found fulfilment in giving to others. I found that by giving hope and comfort to others, I received much in return. Instead of thinking about my own tragedy, I was becoming more concerned about others. My time was not wasted any longer in self-pity. Forgetting myself, I ended up finding myself!

I had a list of people I was praying for during my meditation. The list grew longer as more people were in need of help. Most of them were not aware of my prayers and I did not always know whether their condition improved, but I felt that I would leave it with God. I continued doing the 'absent healing' prayers for a number of years. Little did I know then that I was being led to what turned out to be my commitment to heal the sick by laying on of hands.

I am frequently asked how I knew that I had a gift for healing. Truthfully, I did not know or realise it until my mother arrived in 1975 on a visit from Israel. She was then about 68 years old. She told me that she had been suffering great pain in her knees, and, as she lived in a flat on the third floor, she found it difficult to go up the forty stairs. Her doctor offered no hope, telling her it was 'wear and tear' and what else could she expect at her age? The only thing he could offer was a painkilling drug. My mother refused to take these and decided that she had to live with her condition.

I told her I would look in the 'Psychic News' for a local healer, and indeed I found an address of a group of healers in Hendon, about twenty minutes drive from my home in Harrow. We went there one evening, and while my mother was taken into the room, I waited for her in the corridor.

After the first healing session she already felt an improvement. After the second visit her pain had almost gone. We went for a third time to make sure that the pain had completely disappeared. Indeed, after that short course of healing, my mother had no more problems with her knees, until the day she passed on at the age of 93! It was over twenty years since she had first received healing.

On my mother's third and last visit to the healers, I decided to have healing myself as I was troubled by a noise in my ear – a condition called Tinnitus – which I was told by the doctor was medically incurable. Whilst receiving healing from a lovely lady called Renée, she suddenly told me that I also had the healing gift. I looked at her in disbelief, as I could not accept it. She asked me to stay until after the healing was over and have a cup of tea with her and two other healers. She again insisted that I had the gift of healing and asked me if I would join them, saying that they were moving away from Hendon to Renée's house in Neasden, and would I please come? I promised I would come to help.

On the first evening I arrived, a blessing was offered by a Spiritualist Medium, Mrs. Smart. I told Renée that I would gladly help by doing the job of a receptionist but she would not agree. She asked me to stand behind the patients and put my hands on their shoulders during the healing, while Renée sat in front holding their hands, passing her energy to the patient. I did what she told me rather reluctantly, feeling a sort of a fake, definitely not convinced that I had the healing gift. I felt I was deceiving the people and mentioned it to Renée later. She told me to trust her and do as she asked.

We worked together every Monday evening. I tried to concentrate and pray as I laid my hands on each patient. I could not feel anything. I felt I was wasting my time pretending. One day Renée was unwell and could not come downstairs to the healing session. Her husband asked me to attend to the patients on my own. I was taken aback but could not refuse.

When the first patient came in and sat down, he said that he had a lot of pain in his lower back. I kept my hands on his back for a few minutes when suddenly he pulled my hands away and examined them. He said he thought I had used an ice pack as he felt a freezing sensation in his lower back where the pain was located. He was astonished to feel that the temperature of my hands was normal and that I had no ice pack in my hands!

We were both obviously puzzled. I then put my hands back onto the spot where he had the pain and once again he felt the same freezing sensation. I asked him what the doctor had said about his condition. He said the doctor told him that he had an inflammation in this area. When later I mentioned the case to a friend of mine, a nurse, she said that an ice pack is the most appropriate treatment for this condition! I was glad when it was all over, praying that next week Renée would be well enough to do the healing herself.

The following week I was surprised to be told by the man who had felt the freezing sensation that the pain had almost gone, and that he was now able to climb the stairs without difficulty. Renée, who was present, heard him and reminded me that she had been right about my gift of healing. The incident still did not dispel my doubts. However I decided to give it a fair chance. If it was God's will that I should do this, then I would continue, whether I believed it or not. After all, it was not my doing anyway. I did not seek it or decide to do it. Renée explained to me that I was meant to be a channel for God's energy.

Our healing work continued in Renée's house for about two years. By then I had totally committed myself to it. Although I felt a compulsion to do the healing work, I must admit that at times I felt like staying at home and not going out in the evening, especially in the winter when it was cold, dark or snowing, but I did not give in to this, as I felt that I would be letting down someone in need.

After approximately two years of healing with Renée, who was the most angelic person I had ever met, the healing sessions in her house ceased as sadly she had passed away. I wondered what would happen to my healing work. I waited for further guidance.

Sure enough, a fortnight later, I received a telephone call from George, one of the healers in Renée's group, telling me that he had spoken with the lady in charge of the healing group in a Spiritualist Church in Harrow, who wanted me to join them.

In the meantime without my knowledge, George had written to The National Federation of Spiritual Healers of Great Britain, applying for a certificate for me. He had given them the names of three people who had been successfully healed through me, and they were requested to write a report back to the Federation giving details of their ailments and how long they had been free of their illness. A short while after this I received a certificate from the Federation stating that I was now a Practising Healer – this was 14th November 1977.

I remembered the poem of George Jessop, the healer. What was predicted seemed now to be unfolding, as if according to a plan. But it took many cases and remarkable results finally to convince me of the power of healing directed through me.

I worked as a healer at Vaughan Road Spiritualist Church in Harrow for twelve years. I prayed to God that I might see a real miracle, a case that doctors had given up, a truly hopeless case. Such a case, such a person, came to me.

A woman with a very ill daughter, three years old, came to our house. I welcomed her and enquired about the child's problem. She told me her daughter was gravely ill, with a malignant brain tumour. The doctors said there was nothing further they could do to save her, and that she had only a short time to live, perhaps a few weeks or a few months at the most. Meanwhile, the child was on strong drugs, even heroin, to relieve the agonising pain. Helen (the mother) told me that she was pregnant again as she wanted another baby when her sick child, named Shivone, passed away. She told me that when the child was having these terrible pains she would scream the house down and, in order not to wake up the rest of the family, Helen would take her into the garden, holding her over her shoulder as she was so heavy. While she held her, the child would bite into her shoulders because of the excruciating pain. Helen showed me the lumps and swelling from these bites.

My heart went out to this mother and child. I thought, "O! God! This is too serious a case for me to handle. I'm only a novice healer, I can't take this responsibility as the baby's life is hanging on a thread". Suddenly I remembered an article in the 'Psychic News' about a healer in Italy through whom many miracles were said to have happened. I could not remember the name or place or any details of this healer, but I told Helen that I would immediately make enquiries, and if I traced this healer, would she be willing to travel to Italy even though nothing could be guaranteed, but it was a chance worth taking. Helen said that she was prepared to go anywhere in the world to save her daughter's life, even if she had to sell everything she owned.

I traced the healer after much effort. Her name was Maria Giorgini, called affectionately by all who knew her as 'Mama'. We later learned that 'Mama' had been a doctor before becoming a healer, giving up conventional practice to combine her healing gift with homeopathic and herbal medicine.

I telephoned Helen and gave her the good news. She was overjoyed as she had great faith that 'Mama' would heal her daughter. She made the necessary travel arrangements and went to San Baronto near Pisa. 'Mama' took one look at the child, and, with the little English she knew, she, told Helen exactly what was wrong with her daughter before Helen said anything.

'Mama' told Helen, "Your child will be cured, but it will take three years". She touched and held the little girl, blessed her and gave the appropriate herbal plants to give her in conjunction with whatever medicine she was taking from the doctor in England. One herb was to be fermented in wine for 48 hours, sieved, and given several times a day. Other herbs were to be given less frequently.

'Mama' suggested Helen should bring Shivone to see her every three months to keep up the healing. Helen said she would do so and was convinced 'Mama' would cure her daughter. Not long after giving her daughter the remedies as 'Mama' had instructed, Shivone's pains gradually became less severe.

Slowly, noticeable improvement began to take place. After a few months, Helen took Shivone to the doctor for her check-up and told him about the healing and herbal treatment she was giving her daughter. The doctor was amazed at the improvement in Shivone's condition. Helen felt he thought that it was only a temporary remission. He had previously said that the child would never walk as the tumour was spreading and eventually she would become an invalid, even if she lived beyond the few months he had predicted.

Shivone's improvement continued as mother and daughter returned to see 'Mama' every three months. By now, the doctor stopped the strong drugs as the child was getting better and suffered no more pain. Meanwhile, Helen was well advanced in her pregnancy that made trips to Italy difficult. However this did not lessen her determination to save her daughter and she carried Shivone with great difficulty to the remote hilltop of San Baronto. To our joy and amazement, Shivone began to look more normal, smiling, eating, responding to her surroundings, as any other little girl would, the only problem being that her speech was slow. However, she was receiving speech therapy to help with that.

At the end of three years, and many trips to Italy, Shivone grew up to be a healthy and happy little girl, going to school and leading a normal life. Meanwhile Helen gave birth to a little girl, uncannily born on exactly the same day as Shivone! Helen named the baby after 'Mama's Christian name, Giorgina. Helen's dedication and unwavering faith were well rewarded. The doctors and nurses called Shivone's cure 'miraculous', She had two or three x-rays at intervals and all the medical team had to admit that the malignant tumour had receded and was no longer metastatic. They could not understand it. All they could say was "It is just one of those things", and that she was a very 'lucky' girl.

On many occasions Helen told me "I don't know what made me pick up the local paper and find you. If I hadn't come to you, my child would have died". So what could have been a tragedy ended in joy. Years later, I heard from Helen that Shivone was a 22 year-old young lady and in good health.

I had asked for a miracle, and a miracle had taken place. I was not the healer, only the instrument to direct Helen to the healer who saved her daughter's life. By now I was convinced that when our prayers are intense, unceasing, emerging from the depths of the heart, God listens and helps. Shivone's miracle gave me the confidence and the will to continue on the path of spiritual healing to which I had been led.

At times I was able to help people who were very much in the public eye. Such a person was the sweet-natured ballerina of The Royal Ballet, Covent Garden, wife of the celebrated ballet star Michael Somes. She wrote as follows.

> *"I believe that I owed my continued career as a principal ballerina, with the Royal Ballet Company, dancing at the Royal Opera House, Covent Garden, to Ruth's loving spiritual healing. In 1979 I broke not one, but both wrists in a fall on stage in the middle of a performance as the Young Girl in Sir Fredrick Ashton's 'The Two Pigeons'.*
>
> *I entered the Harrow Spiritualist Church with both wrists in plaster up to the elbow, and was introduced to a group of healers, Ruth being the chosen one. When Ruth began to heal, almost immediately I felt an electric sensation shooting*

through the plaster into my wrists. This led to Ruth suggesting that I should come and see her at her home to have extra healing. There I felt an even greater sensation so strong like 'pins and needles' going through the wrists and into the fingers. I knew in my heart that the wrists were healed. With great difficulty I managed to persuade the surgeon to remove the plaster three weeks earlier than was originally suggested, saying that if I was wrong they could replace them. To the staff's amazement, they were completely healed, and a perfect shape, as they had been compound fractures, looking like a bent spoon.

It was not many weeks after that I was back dancing Princess Aurora in the Sleeping Beauty, all thanks to Ruth's deepest love of her spiritual work.

Wendy Ellis Somes
London

Wendy and I have become very close friends and are in constant touch with each other.

In 1984 a young mother, named Anita, brought her little four year-old son Terence, to me for healing. For a whole year Terence had suffered excruciating pain in his left arm. He could not move the arm at all. The doctor could not help, nor could the hospital. Painkillers achieved little and an exploratory operation was suggested. Poor Terence could not sleep at night, as the slightest touch on his arm would awaken him with unbearable pain. Anita was at a loss as to what to do. She and her husband Bunny were very much against an operation. And so a whole year went by with no respite from the pain.

Eventually Anita's sister-in-law Dulcie, who came regularly for healing, suggested Anita should bring Terence too. When the child was brought to me I looked at his beautiful sweet face and he captured my heart. There was such an outpouring of love going to him while I gave him healing. I kept my hand an inch or two above his left arm, avoiding touching him for fear of causing pain.

At the end of the healing I told Anita to bring Terence back next week. The following day Anita telephoned informing me that Terence woke up the next morning waving his arm and repeating joyfully, "My arm is alright, and my arm doesn't hurt any more!"

Anita could not believe her eyes or ears. I listened to what she said in astonishment. I was dumbfounded. I had only seen the child once. I told her to bring Terence to my house. She promised to come with Terence and her husband Bunny on Sunday.

Sunday arrived, the doorbell rang and little Terence walked in waving his arm to show me that he was now fine. I cannot describe how I felt when I saw him walking in with a big smile on his adorable face. I hugged him and put him on my lap. I could now touch him without fear of hurting him.

We all were elated and overjoyed because a year of suffering had come to an end. Anita continued to bring Terence for healing for three months, 'to be on the safe side'. To this day Terence, now over 20 years old, has never felt a twitch of a pain and has been going to the gym, taking part in all sports activities. The pain never returned! The family happily adopted me, and we keep in touch to this day. It is a source of great joy for me to see them all, especially Terence, who gives me a big hug and a kiss. There is a special bond between the family and me.

In describing a few remarkable cases, which have left a strong impression on my mind and have given me feelings of immense joy, I remember yet another wonderful case. It happened whilst I was at the Spiritualist Church in Harrow on a Tuesday evening in about 1983 or 1984.

A nice-looking young man brought Denise, a young lady aged about 25 years old to me. She was in a wheelchair. He lifted her out of the wheelchair, and sat her on the chair facing me. The young woman seemed to be severely disabled. She also had curvature of the spine. She could not sit upright. Her chin almost touched her chest. She told me that she had been born with a serious bone condition.

For years she had been in and out of hospital, having to endure many operations and treatments, but all to no avail.

She was paralysed from the waist down. She did not have much feeling in her hands either and because of that had to use a thermometer to gauge the temperature of the water before taking a bath; otherwise she risked scalding herself. It was truly a sad and heart–rending case.

She mentioned that the young man who came with her, whom I thought might have been her brother, was, in fact, her boyfriend. They had met at an archery event for disabled people where he was a spectator. She said that they were engaged and planned to get married sometime in the future. She also related to me that the doctors told her that she would spend the rest of her life in a wheelchair, and that she could never have children.

Having met Ian, this fine and healthy young man who showed her so much love and devotion, her life had been given a new spark of hope and determination. I felt that no matter what her condition, or the doctors' verdict might be, there was always the potent energy of God's love that is beyond all limitations. One has to surrender to that power with prayer and faith.

I laid my hands over this girl's head, then her shoulders, going right down her curved spine. I then took her feet into my hands and held them for at least ten minutes. Denise continued to come weekly for healing and after the first four or five sessions she suddenly, with a smile on her face, said that she could feel a little heat and slight vibration in her feet! I looked at her surprised and with a flutter of elation in my heart. I took her hands into mine and finished the healing with a prayer of gratitude. Denise told Ian of the sensation which she had felt and he too had a happy smile, no doubt kindling some hope in both of them.

Denise came regularly for almost a year. My fellow-healers and I could see a positive improvement-taking place. She began to have feeling in her feet and legs, whilst her spine gradually became straighter. Her head was now raised up instead of collapsing down onto her chest. After a few more months she was able to get out of the wheelchair unaided and to sit facing me, without Ian's help. It is impossible to put into words how thrilled and delighted we all were for this lovely young couple. The improvement had prompted them to set their wedding date three months ahead.

Denise by now was out of the wheelchair and walking! On their wedding day she walked down the aisle, smiling joyfully to her waiting husband-to-be. I did not see Denise for another two years, though I often wondered how she was and whether they had a child. One day, walking in Harrow Weald, I suddenly saw Denise walking towards me wheeling a pushchair with a young toddler sitting in it. I shouted with delight at seeing them. She told me that she had given birth to a fine, healthy little boy and that she was pregnant and expecting her second child!!! I asked her what the doctors said at the hospital. She smiled and replied that they just shrugged their shoulders in astonishment, commenting, "You are a very lucky girl".

Her recovery, deemed impossible by the medical world, came about through the immense power of love and prayer, of her husband and of the healers, and was truly miraculous. Never abandon hope, never despair, and rely on the great healing power arising from the divine source.

My home life meanwhile continued as before. My husband was more and more engrossed in his business, which was increasingly successful. My daughters and my son Robin were growing fast, and my daily life revolved around caring for my family. But, for me, life now had a new and wider dimension. Helping others had given me a new purpose, a new meaning.

Chapter 4

ELLIOT, ANNE AND THE POWER OF HEALING

"Hands that help are holier than lips that pray"

Sathya Sai Baba

In 1983 I received a telephone call from a lady who introduced herself as Miriam. She hoped I could help her with her only son Elliot, who was twenty-one years old. He was schizophrenic, sometimes violent, hitting her and acting aggressively towards other people. Twice he had tried to commit suicide, once by cutting his wrist, and once by swallowing an overdose of drugs. In spite of injections as well as seeing a psychiatrist regularly, she could see no change in his behaviour. I was her last resort. I was in two minds whether I should take on such a case, but could not ignore her cry for help.

I told Miriam that before I came I needed Elliot's consent, so I asked Elliot on the telephone whether he wanted me to come. He answered with a slight stutter, "Yes". That afternoon I drove to London's West End where they lived.

In the flat Miriam told me that when he was born Elliot had slight brain damage, which caused him to stutter sometimes, and that his co-ordination was not perfect. He could not join with other children at school in physical activities. The children made fun of him because of it. This caused him to become withdrawn. Consequently he suffered from severe depression and a deep-seated inferiority complex. Attempts at treatment in Switzerland and the United States were of no avail. Elliot would not go out of the house except when he was taken by car to the doctor for his injections and to see the psychiatrist. He never wanted to wear clothes and lived in his pyjamas all the time. He was confined to the home for years. A sad and pitiful case.

While we were talking, the door opened slightly, and Elliot's head peeped through. I caught sight of him. I looked straight at him and our eyes met. I gave him a reassuring smile and asked him to come in. Hesitatingly, he walked in, wearing his pyjamas under a dressing gown, and sat down in the armchair facing me. His mother left the room so that Elliot and I could speak freely.

Alone with Elliot, I could see he looked lost in his own world of darkness and despair. I felt instinctively that here was a case where I could not lay my hands on him, as I usually do, so I began to talk to him. I felt his exasperation and pain in my heart, so, while talking, I was mentally surrounding him with light and love. I began telling him about my own deep depression following a car accident, when I wanted to end my life. I had to fight tooth and nail against these feelings of self-destruction and, because of that, I found a spiritual path, which brought me peace and blessings. This enabled me to become a healer. Through my tragedy, I could understand and identify with suffering and therefore was able to help. I told him I was sure there was something for him to do in his life, that he too in turn would help some one through his own experience. I said that something good would eventually come out of something bad, if we but had determination and faith.

He looked at me intently, listening to every word, while sitting on the edge of his chair, anxious and tense. Suddenly as I continued talking, Elliot gave a deep sigh of relief. All tension left him and he sank back into the armchair. Perhaps it was the first time he had let go and relaxed. There were tears in his eyes. I felt that he was relieved, and that here at last he had met someone who understood him.

He began to perceive that he was not alone. I told him I could identify with his struggle. He did not need to tell me – I knew. He became visibly more relaxed as if a heavy load had been lifted off his shoulders. He gave me a shy smile of approval. I kept talking and he seemed to be drinking in every word I uttered. I asked him what he liked doing and if he had any friends. He told me that he liked writing poems and asked immediately if I would like to read them. I said I would love to. Excitedly he got up from his chair, went to the cupboard and brought me his poems. I read a few, while he looked at me intently, perhaps to see my reaction.

I told him how gifted he was, that he should continue to write poems, perhaps publish them, as I was sure people would enjoy reading them. I asked him what kind of music he liked. He answered, "Classical music". I said to him, "Why don't you phone one of your old friends and go to a concert?" He looked at me and said that perhaps he would do that. I told him, "Elliot, there is work for you to do in this world. You too could help someone like I am helping you today. You are intelligent and gifted, and should make use of these qualities". Towards the end he was talking freely, animatedly, even smiling. He had found a friend in me – an equal. I was so moved to see such a change after only three hours of talking with him.

Normally, when healing, I would lay my hands on a person, but there are different kinds of healing. Sometimes, words alone are the most effective forms of healing, as was obvious in this case.

We agreed that I would come again later in the week. The next morning Miriam rang. "Ruth, I don't know what you have done, but, after you left, Elliot went into the kitchen and made me a cup of tea and brought it to me. I could not believe it. He had never done it before; he was always so aggressive to me. He seemed more calm". I said that I was as delighted as she was and that I looked forward to seeing Elliot again in a few days time.

Despite my husband's objections, later that week I went to see Elliot. He opened the door for me with a welcoming smile. My conversation with him continued, I told him about my spiritual path, about the Self Realisation Fellowship and how it had changed my life. He listened attentively to every word I said. I never knew what I was going to say next. The words just flowed. I did not have to think, but whatever I said must have been what he needed to hear. I could see the change-taking place in him. He was calmer and no longer aggressive towards his mother or the daily help, who I was told had been afraid to enter the flat.

After a few more visits the idea came to my mind to try and get Elliot out of his own self-inflicted isolation, to bring him out of the house. I asked him "Would you like to come with your mother for lunch at my home?" He looked surprised but said "Yes" with a smile. I was so happy to hear his positive reply that I called his mother in and told her about it. She looked at me, and then at Elliot, with disbelief, and when she realised that Elliot really meant it, she gave a broad and happy smile. I invited them to come the next day at noon thinking Elliot might change his mind if I left it any longer.

The following morning I prepared everything and waited for Elliot and his mother to arrive. At exactly 12 o'clock they came. I went out to welcome them, and there was Elliot, wearing a suit and a tie! He gave me a plant. I thanked him, commenting how smart he looked. Miriam told me that in the morning Elliot asked her to give him money to buy a suit. She gave him the money and when he came back he had bought himself a suit and a plant for me! She could not believe her eyes.

After lunch, Elliot mentioned that he had contacted a friend and arranged to go to a concert. I was delighted. While talking with Miriam, she told me Elliot had expressed a wish to study the Jewish scriptures, as he felt he wanted to be a Rabbi. I looked at Elliot for confirmation, and he nodded. Miriam said she was looking for someone to teach him privately as she did not think it right for him to enter a college while he was so vulnerable. This was also Elliot's wish and I agreed. I said I hope she could find the right person.

I continued to visit Elliot over a period of six months, once or twice a week. On one of my visits his mother told me that she had found a lady teacher who was blind though highly qualified in theology, and who also spoke four or five languages. Elliot had met and liked her. There was an immediate bond between them. I could see how good it would be for Elliot to study with her. I was told they had already started lessons and he felt protective towards her and wanted to help her in her blindness.

She was an inspiration for him, showing that her blindness was not a barrier to her achieving her aims, and making her life worthwhile. I pondered on the 'coincidence' in finding such a teacher for Elliot! He still needed to go to the doctor for his injections but no longer needed the psychiatrist. He was now coping and doing something positive. He regained his self-esteem and the will to live. I felt more had been achieved than I thought possible. I told Elliot and his mother that I would leave him now to build his life but that if they needed me I would be there for them.

I later received one or two phone calls from Miriam telling me that Elliot was continuing with his studies and was going out with friends. For two years I heard nothing further, but then came a call saying that they had moved to a new flat in London and asked me to come to tea. I took with me a bunch of beautiful roses from my own garden and went to see them.

When I entered, Elliot greeted me with a smile. He was wearing a smart suit. His mother welcomed me with a hug. She said that Elliot was enjoying his studies and was continuing with them. He looked well and happy. His whole life and that of his family had changed for the better. I was so happy for them.

I continued healing at the Harrow Spiritualist Church for about twelve years when some changes took place and I decided to leave. Once again I was waiting for a direction. One evening, about a month later, I received a call from a lady healer friend asking me if I could help in a healing clinic in Pinner as they needed an extra healer there.

I agreed, and on Monday evening for the first time I went to Pinner. I liked the spiritual atmosphere of the group and continued there for six years. In addition, I was directed to a Hindu Shrine, also in Harrow, to which I will refer later, where I was asked to give healing on Sunday afternoons. So for over five years I worked in both places.

I quote a letter I received from Anne Danvers, a young woman whom I helped at my home, but whom I had met at the Sai Baba centre. She wrote:

"I have to admit that like many other people, I resorted to spiritual healing when all else had failed.

It was the summer of '79 when an unsightly lump first appeared on the back of my hand. I have no recollection of the original trauma that caused its formation. It was about the size of a walnut and was actually a cyst connected to a tendon on the wrist.

Two methods are available for the removal of ganglions. The traditional remedy was a sharp thump with a heavy object – usually the family bible. The alternative method was surgery. It was a good twelve years before I opted for the latter.

There was, however, a third option available to me, a far gentler one, and this was pointed out to me a week before the operation by Mr. Patel (of the Hindu centre). A group of dedicated healers were offering their services from his home on Sunday afternoons and he assured me that after a couple of sessions with one of them the ganglion would dissolve.

I knew that this would be less painful than surgery, but after months of being on the NHS waiting list I decided to go ahead with the operation and the ganglion was duly excised.

All was well for six months and my hand was back to normal. Then the ganglion reappeared, this time it was even larger. I allowed another year to elapse before I finally approached one of the healers, who is also a dear friend.

Although I knew that Ruth was a powerful healer who had effected many cures, I was still not fully convinced that she could rid me of this horrible lump! And I'm sorry to say that I walked into her healing sanctuary in July 1993 with more scepticism than faith! My doubts were reinforced when I did not experience any heat emanating from her hands as she held them over me, nor were there any other signs that healing was taking place.

Imagine my astonishment when a day or two later I noticed that the ganglion had changed in size and appearance. Previously round and firm, it was now becoming increasingly flat and flaccid!

I had a second healing session with Ruth a week later and in the days that followed, the ganglion became flatter. It turned to fluid and then it gradually dissolved until it totally and finally disappeared!

Ruth was as amazed and delighted as I was, and although she takes no credit for it, I shall always be grateful to her for being such a wonderful channel, and I would like to take this opportunity to express my heartfelt thanks!"

Anne
Bushey, London

My ability to heal is not unique. A healer is an ordinary person, but one with a strong and sincere desire to heal, a heart filled with love and compassion, and a readiness to serve. God does the rest. And so Anne was healed.

I feel privileged to have been able to help many people over the years. I cannot think of greater joy than, when someone comes in agony, mental, physical or emotional, and returns the following week with a smile and a new positive attitude. To hear that he or she had felt the benefit of the healing power, inducing a happier frame of mind, has always given me a feeling of elation that far exceeds anything the material world could offer. To feel such a joy is a gift for which I am deeply grateful, and my life has become more meaningful and fulfilling as a result.

In so many successful cases the patient became a dear friend, in some instances as close as family, and thus my circle of friends has grown and grown over the years, greatly enriching my life.

Chapter 5

MEANWHILE, AT HOME...

"Come just one step towards me I shall come a hundred towards you. Shed just one tear and I shall wipe a hundred from your eyes."

Sathya Sai Baba

My husband had no interest in my healing work, my spiritual quest, or my periods of meditation. In fact, just the reverse. He used to mock me and make fun of my spiritual interests. He did not even want to hear about the people I had helped. He was immersed in business and material things. His aim was to make as much money as he could. He felt this would give him power and the respect of others. And so our paths gradually began to diverge.

In solely material terms, we lived a very good life. His business prospered, we were short of nothing. We had a beautiful home, luxurious holidays, cars, designer clothes, whatever one's heart could desire. This satisfied him, but deep down I knew this was not my road, but I said nothing.

Following my accident in 1961, our daughter Diana had been sent to a farm to recover from the shock of the ordeal.

Whilst there she learnt to ride ponies and show-jump. She took to it very quickly and proved to be a natural rider. When she returned home from the farm, all she wanted was to be with horses.

When we realised how serious she was about riding, we bought her her first pony for show jumping, which we put at livery at the riding stables. We soon came to the decision that we should move house to be nearer the stables as it was clear to us that this was not a passing fancy, but something she was very serious about pursuing as a career. As a result, we had a lovely home built in Harrow closer to the riding stables Diana attended. We also built stables in the grounds of our new home.

Our life centred around horse shows, and my husband found in our daughter's career a hobby to involve him in. We were proud of Diana's success, as she won quite a number of events including some major trophies. At seventeen, Diana obtained her driving licence and used to drive her large horsebox with the horses to shows with her father and the groom accompanying her. I would join them when shows were closer to home.

One day just at the start of the show jumping season, Diana's best horse cut his leg on the fence whilst in the fields. The cut was very deep, almost touching the bone. The vet said that it would take a good few months to heal which meant that she would have to miss the whole show-jumping season.

Needless to say, Diana was heartbroken and depressed. We decided to send her away on holiday to my mother in Israel. While there, she met a handsome young man called Arik. They fell in love and she came back home bringing Arik with her.

They decided to get married and live in Israel. My husband was particularly unhappy about it, as Diana was the apple of his eye and he did not want her to go so far from home. However, he eventually had to give in. The wedding took place in Haifa, Israel, and we all went there for the special day. They wanted to settle in Israel so we bought them a flat near Tel-Aviv and left them to get on with their married life.

After barely a year away, Diana felt homesick and wanted to come back to England. They sold the flat, returned home and bought a house near us. A few months after they had returned, to my great surprise I found that I was expecting my third child at the age of 42. It was also just a few months before our 25th wedding anniversary.

Our son Robin was born on 4th March 1970, four months before Diana gave birth to our first grandson Jeremy on 16th July 1970. Diana and Arik's second son, Alex, was born about three years later on 30th July 1973.

A few months after the birth of Alex, Arik began to complain of not feeling well; he had bad headaches and was coughing a lot. The doctor dismissed his complaint, saying he was a young man and there was nothing wrong with him. Within a few months Arik started spitting blood when coughing and was rushed into hospital.

It was discovered that he had a form of stomach cancer that had spread to his lungs. He underwent an emergency operation but following that operation the spread of the cancer was rapid. Within a few days Arik died. He was only twenty-nine, leaving Diana a widow of twenty-seven with two young children aged four years and under one year. Needless to say how low and depressed she felt.

Harry, a nearby neighbour, twenty-one years older than Diana, whose wife had recently died, was also left with two children. Soon Diana and Harry started going out together, and found much in common. They both were in the same situation, and obviously needed each other. After barely a few months they got married. We organized the reception in our home with just the family and close friends.

Harry's work took him first to Hong Kong, where Diana now had to cope with four children in a strange country. They lived on the 17th floor of a skyscraper where she was very unhappy. Later his work took him to Germany. There they had a nice villa with a garden and Diana seemed to be happier.

I visited Diana in both Hong Kong and Germany. After two years in Germany they came back to England and stayed together for some months, after which they acknowledged the marriage was not working and they separated amicably.

I was very sorry for my daughter. Life, which had seemed so good for her at first, had taken a tragic turn, and at such a young age to be both widowed and divorced was sad indeed. Yet, having helped and healed others, there was little I could do to help my daughter except to support her in her problems and to pray for her.

Chapter 6

JOURNEY TO SELF REALISATION

Value and purity are not rooted in weakness.
Rather, they are strong qualities that fight
the forces of evil.

Paramahansa Yogananda

I had been following the teachings of Paramahansa Yogananda for some years, and found as a result more peace than I had ever felt, more understanding of life, more patience and tolerance of people and events. Suddenly one bright morning I was taken aback with shock and disbelief when my husband, who could never understand nor tolerate my interest in the spiritual path I was following, uttered the words: - "I think the Self-Realisation Fellowship has done you a lot of good. If you want to go to the Retreat I will arrange your flight!"

These words took a little while to sink in. I wondered whether he really meant it. When I realised he was serious, my heart leapt with joy and anticipation and I started counting the days to my trip. Little did I suspect at the time that my husband had his own reasons for wanting me on the other side of the Atlantic.

I felt Yogananda's teachings had helped me through years of personal and emotional trials. I had been lost in the wilderness of a material life and was unsure which way to turn. I tried to meditate but could not do this regularly. I began to lose the rhythm of the meditation technique, which I learnt in the lessons sent to me from his organisation. I tried to follow another spiritual path, Transcendental Meditation by the Maharishi Mahesh Yogi, which was simpler and less demanding, but I could find neither depth nor peace in it – it was not for me. Master Yogananda must have watched over me through these spiritually barren and wandering years and brought me back into the fold by making this trip possible.

July 1979

The day finally arrived, when I set foot on the plane for my first pilgrimage to the Self-Realisation Convention and Retreat in California, founded by the Saintly Yogi, Paramahansa Yogananda. He was one of the first Masters to travel to the West from India in 1920 to teach yoga and meditation and to awaken sleeping souls to spirituality. My journey was the realisation of a dream.

I was full of happy anticipation. I knew the flight would take about eleven hours and for me the only way to pass the time was to read one of Paramahansa's books which I had brought with me. Once immersed in reading I knew time would pass quickly.

A few hours into the flight I happened to glance out of the window. I was awe-struck by the breathtaking view of snow-covered mountains surrounded by the sea below. What amazed me was the blanket of white dots of different shapes and sizes, which I was told, were floating icebergs. I asked the steward over which part of the world we were flying and he said we were over Iceland. My eyes were transfixed at the beauty of this scenery.

After Iceland came Greenland. I looked down and was surprised to see that the mountaintops were bare of snow that must have melted. The peaks of the bare mountains were brown in colour. My eyes were suddenly caught by one particular mountain with a flat rounded top, rather like a plateau, on which I saw a large letter 'R' as if it had been engraved there, in silver. The letter 'R' was shining and reflecting shimmering rays of light. It was strange to see and I wondered what it could mean. Was this shimmering sight a sign of special significance that was personal to me, as it was the first letter of my name? Was someone telling me that I was not alone, as this was the first time I had travelled on my own to such a far and unknown place? Little did I know how much I was to need help and protection before my travels were over.

The plane landed in Los Angeles Airport in the afternoon. I now had to find a way of getting to the Retreat in Encinitas, which I thought was near Los Angeles. I asked one of the people at the airport how I could get to Encinitas and he said that there was a coach terminal nearby and that I should look for the one with Encinitas written on it. I came off the plane tired and drained after an eleven-hour flight. I was carrying my luggage with difficulty while looking for the coach terminal.

As I arrived there I found the coach, which went to Encinitas. I got on, paid my fare and sat down. I asked the driver how long the journey would take and he replied four to five hours! It was now 4 p.m. I had neither eaten nor drunk since the last meal on the plane, which was several hours earlier.

An hour went by before the coach finally started moving. I lay back in my seat and looked forward to getting to the Retreat, to have something to eat and a good night's sleep. The coach trip seemed to be endless, stopping at every town and village with people getting on and off. It began to seem as though I would never get to my destination. By now it was beginning to get dark, as day turned into night, without any sign as yet of 'Encinitas'. I looked at my watch. The time was 11 p.m. I was getting worried about arriving in a strange town in darkness, especially since I still had to find my way to the Retreat. I looked around. I was the only one left on the coach. Finally, I heard the driver call out "Encinitas", I looked again at my watch – it was 11.30 p.m. I staggered off the coach, exhausted, thirsty and hungry. It was by now about ten hours since my last meal on the plane and some 18 hours since leaving London.

Alighting from the coach, all I could see was pitch darkness, except for some light coming from a liquor shop. It was indeed a ghost town and gave me an eerie feeling.

I entered the liquor shop, asking for the direction to the Self Realization Retreat. The shop assistant was unfriendly, and did not want to help. Eventually, after much pleading with him, with tears in my eyes, he looked up the Directory and phoned to the Retreat telling them of my arrival and the location of his shop.

While I was waiting in the shop, two weird, scruffy and drunk men walked in looking to buy more drinks. The shop assistant told me to get out of the shop, as it was midnight and he was closing down. As I left the shop, the lights were switched off. Once again I was all alone in pitch darkness, scared and in a panic. I feared the two drunken men who had left the shop would come back for me. There was not a soul around, I was an easy prey.

As I sat on my suitcase crying and praying, a voice from above the liquor shop called asking if I needed help. I explained that I needed to get to the Self Realization Retreat. He said he knew the place and offered to take me there.

As no one arrived from the Retreat, I had no choice but to put my trust in this man. He was unshaven, with long hair and looked like a hippy.

He told me to climb into his van, putting my suitcase at the back. I sat beside him. His van smelled foul. I wondered whether it was a smell of drugs. I was frightened and felt in danger, as my life was in his hands. I prayed to God to watch over me and bring me safely to the Retreat.

Thankfully, and by the Grace of God, he dropped me at the Retreat's gate, where two nuns met me. I breathed a sigh of relief. So did the nuns, who told me how worried they were for my safety, and welcomed me warmly.

When showing me to my room, they told me of their concern. They explained that there were many drug addicts in the area and on many occasions dead bodies were found in the morning in isolated grounds in the surrounding area.

They had been convinced that I had been killed. I could understand then their look of astonishment on seeing me. They said it was God and Master who protected me, and it was a miracle that I had turned up alive!

They brought me food and drink, which I relished after fifteen hours of fasting. I was touched by the love and kindness of these nuns who were like angels making me feel safe and at home. I had a quick shower and fell asleep as soon as my head touched the pillow.

First Day

I woke up to the sound of a bell at 6.a.m. feeling surprisingly refreshed although I had had only a few hours sleep. I knew from the programme that at 6.30 a.m. there were fifteen minutes of energising exercises in the courtyard. I quickly washed, dressed, and went down to join the group. There were about twenty of us men and women

. After the exercises we went into the temple for about half an hour's meditation and devotional singing, after which we had breakfast in the dining room. Everything was spotlessly clean. The resident nuns prepared the breakfast. Most of the vegetables and some of the fruits were homegrown in the grounds of the Retreat. No wonder everything tasted so delicious.

After breakfast, I explored the surroundings. The Retreat was built on a high cliff with a view of the Pacific Ocean stretching to the far horizon. The picturesque gardens with multi-coloured flowers, shrubs and trees as well as streams and ponds with lilies, ducks and swans floating on the water made a delightful sight. Among the shrubs and flowers were benches where one could sit and read, meditate or just enjoy the breathtaking view and tranquillity of the place.

Its sense of peace was balm to my troubled soul. This spot was truly heaven on earth. I felt transported into a different dimension. The world outside with all its problems and strife ceased to exist. In the grounds people were strolling silently, sitting on the benches, reading or meditating. If one had to talk it was in a whisper. One did not feel the need to talk, just to try and be with their inner self.

While walking, I found a spot where there was an enormous tree spreading its wide branches, providing shade over a large area. To the thick trunk of the tree was attached a carved wooden statue of the much-loved St. Francis of Assisi. Under the shade of these benevolent branches and leaves were two semi-circular benches placed in front of St. Francis so that one could sit and focus on the Saint and meditate. As I looked at St. Francis I felt so moved by the vibrations of holiness and gentleness coming from him, I was unable to control the tears rolling down my face. I sat down to meditate and take in these beautiful vibrations.

It was strange that every day when I came to this spot and looked at St. Francis I would be overcome by this emotion. I cannot find an explanation for this, only that perhaps it was because the beauty of his soul merging with the surrounding beauty had overwhelmed me in that way. One of the devotees from Holland whom I got to know noticed this and remarked on it. At the end of her stay when we parted, we exchanged addresses. How surprised and moved I was to receive from her a couple of months later a parcel with an exquisitely carved statue of St. Francis of Assisi with doves resting in his hand. I treasure this little statue to this day.

I stayed at the Retreat for ten days – ten memorable days. The nuns were the embodiment of love, peace and selfless service. I so much wished I could stay there forever. Sadly, time had come to bid farewell to this unforgettable Retreat and get back into the 'hurly burly' of the material world.

On my return home life resumed its old pattern. It was a painful change from heaven to the noisy hell of everyday life. However, something of what I gained at this Retreat had remained with me. For a while I felt recharged and uplifted. I could recapture the feeling of the peace, which I experienced in that tranquil place. I was better able to cope with the problems and difficult situation in which I now found myself. I was more tolerant, more patient.

At the back of my mind I was yearning to return to that abode of love and peace. I felt a great need to be in the spiritual environment again. And return I finally did when I boarded the plane for my second trip to the Self-Realisation Fellowship for the 1981 Convocation and retreat. This time I first visited my sister Miki in Atlanta for a few days before going on to the Convocation in Los Angeles.

While with my sister, I received a telephone call from my husband. After chatting for a few seconds, he cut short our conversation and said that he was passing the telephone to the 'au pair' to say a few words, not asking first if I wished to speak to her. I was annoyed that we could not have a private conversation without her being present even during a long distance call. When I put the phone down, Miki, who was standing next to me, said that she had a feeling, in fact she was almost sure, that there was 'something going on' between my husband and the 'au pair'.

I said that although I did not like her familiarity with my husband, I thought that it might only be paternal feelings between them, as she missed her father and family, bearing in mind that she was about eight years younger than our daughter Diana, and thirty six years younger than my husband. However, I remembered that this thought had crossed my mind when my husband had suddenly offered to buy me a ticket to U.S.A, go to the Retreat, but I quickly dismissed the thought. I felt that our marriage was secure with nearly forty years behind us three children, and four grandchildren. My husband throughout our marriage was madly in love with me, jealous and over-possessive, the cause of many arguments. I therefore did not think that this young woman had a chance of breaking up our marriage. She would soon have to return back to her country and that would be the end of it.

How wrong I was. Miki lifted the self-imposed veil from my eyes, saying, "Ruth, don't be so naïve. Open your eyes on your return". The next day I said farewell to my sister and boarded the plane to the Convocation and Retreat in Los Angeles.

On arrival I checked into the Biltmore Hotel where the Convocation was to take place. The first meeting was going to be in the evening, which left me enough time to unpack, refresh myself and go down to the restaurant. As I looked around I saw many devotees sitting, talking quietly with each other. I sat at a table on my own and was soon joined by a young lady from New York. It was also her first trip to the Convocation.

We felt an immediate affinity as though we had been old friends. We were soon sharing our spiritual experiences recounting how we came to find our Guru Yogananda. It is always fascinating to hear how each one is guided in different ways and in various circumstances to find his or her Guru. How true is the saying "When the pupil is ready – the Master appears".

We entered the large hall and sat in the fourth or fifth row. On the stage was a large photograph of Paramahansa

Yogananda decorated with garlands of multicoloured flowers. On either side of his photograph were baskets of beautiful flower arrangements as well as near the chair where the President of SRF, Sri Daya Mata, was to sit.

I looked around as the hall began to fill. I could see the multitude of faces from every country, every background and nationality. There was an atmosphere of unity and the feeling of belonging to a 'world family'. It was as if all the different labels of religions, castes or creeds had melted away. Here we were all brothers and sisters following the spiritual path of Divine Love and Service as taught and exemplified by our saintly Guru Paramahansa Yogananda. I had never experienced such a feeling of unity and harmony. There was this immediate bond of friendship between all of us which was so wonderful.

I noticed that a few of the monks and nuns were already on the platform. The meeting was about to begin; the hall fell into complete silence. One of the monks opened the Convocation with warm words of welcome. He said that the SRF Headquarters Mother Centre was our spiritual home and that we should feel free to come any time and enjoy the peaceful vibrations of the grounds.

There followed a lecture on Yogananda's teachings and the technique of meditation, which is meant to expand awareness beyond the limitations of body and mind, enabling one to commune with God and experience the joy of uniting oneself with His Omnipresent consciousness. We sang devotional songs and the feeling of love and fraternity was uplifting. We seemed to be in a different world, united by our love of God who is the Father of us all. We were fortunate to see the Light of Truth while the world outside seemed to be in the darkness of ignorance, the cause of hatred, intolerance, jealousies and wars.

> *"Body, mind and soul are interrelated", the Master said. "You have a duty to the body – keeping it fit, a duty to the mind – developing its powers; and a duty to the soul – daily meditation on the Source of your being. If you fulfil your duty to the soul, body and mind will benefit, too; but if you neglect the soul, eventually body and mind also will suffer."*
>
> *Paramahansa Yogananda*

We went to visit Mount Washington, the Mother Centre. There we were warmly welcomed by smiling nuns in white saris, serene and angelic. In the middle of the immaculate green lawns were tables covered with orange coloured silk material gathered and falling into pleats held by a colourful band pinned to the top edge of the table. Above was a colourful canopy giving shade from the hot sun. Altogether, it made a cheerful and delightful sight, truly a joyful homecoming atmosphere.

There was cool refreshing fruit juice pouring out of a fountain standing at the centre of the table, which tasted like nectar. We entered the building where Yogananda had lived. We were shown his private rooms where everything was left as it was on his last day. One could feel the holy vibration in every part of this delightful home. In fact, all the places that Yogananda had blessed with his presence have an almost tangible spiritual stillness to them, a balm to the soul.

After our tour of the home and surroundings, we sat in the temple for a short while, most of us meditating or just deep in thought. I opened my eyes and noticed Sri Daya Mata the SRF President walking slowly down the aisle. When Daya Mata walked just a few yards from me I was in awe. There was a sweet smile on her face, so much love in that smile; she seemed to emanate pure saintliness. Many of us had tears in our eyes, tears of joy at the privilege of having her amongst us. She walked onto the platform and sat on the chair beside the large photograph of her beloved Master Yogananda.

Daya Mata greeted us in a warm and gentle voice. She spoke about Yogananda and his teachings, relating personal experiences with her beloved Guru. She led us into a short meditation of about fifteen minutes, after which, at the door she shook hands and spoke with each of us. We walked out into the garden, uplifted, and elated. We felt privileged and blessed.

As we strolled in the grounds, we were told that our small group of six people from London would have a special private interview with Sri Daya Mata that afternoon. We could hardly believe our luck. As we had time to spare, I went to the bookshop and bought the book 'Autobiography of a Yogi', even though I had a copy at home, as I wanted Daya Mata to sign it. I also bought a photograph of Yogananda hoping she would sign that too.

Later we were shown into the cosy study where Sri Daya Mata received people for private interviews. We sat quietly awaiting her. The door opened, and there was Sri Daya Mata, in her orange sari, smiling sweetly at us as she entered the room. She greeted us warmly and sat down. We all sat in a semi-circle in front of her on the floor. She spoke to us about Yogananda's teachings, his thoughts regarding problems in the world, also words of wisdom on family relationships, problems with children, and how to deal with them. It was most enlightening. She asked if we had any questions. A few in the group sought some explanations of the teachings, which she responded to in clear and illuminating terms.

It was a joy and special privilege to be so close to Daya Mata. We felt we were surrounded by the love and peace emanating from her. The interview came to a close and Daya Mata got up, opened the door, seeing us out one by one, and again exchanging a few words with each of us, inviting us to come again whenever we wished – "It is your home too" – she said in her quiet gentle voice. As my turn came I gave her the book asking her if she would sign it for me. She happily obliged, as well as signing Yogananda's photograph. She held my Japamala beads in her hands and blessed them, for which I was overjoyed and grateful.

I followed the group into the garden. We walked slowly, not speaking, but each deep in thought. What a wonderful, unbelievable day we had had. While walking we came to the 'Meditation Tree', the tree Yogananda used to sit under and meditate. There were benches around the tree for devotees to sit and feel the special vibrations of that spot. We quietly discussed and exchanged our impressions of what we understood from Daya Mata's explanations.

Back on the coach, we visited other places of pilgrimage founded by Paramahansa Yogananda, equally beautiful and peaceful. We returned to the hotel, a tired but happy group. Many were leaving for home the next day. We said our goodbyes, and exchanged addresses, and promised to write.

I spent one week listening to lectures at the Convocation and then returned to the retreat at Encinita for the remaining week. The experience filled me with renewed determination to try harder and be more consistent in my meditation back home. We all felt we had greatly benefited from the Convocation and the contact we had made with each other.

On arrival at Heathrow Airport my husband and eleven-year-old son Robin were waiting for me and drove me home. I soon got back to the usual everyday routine, whilst still feeling within me the spiritual strength, which I had received at the Convocation and Retreat. It helped me to see things in a different light. I had different priorities and my values had changed. Things which used to irritate or upset me did not affect me in the same way anymore. I felt more detached, stronger, and altogether more self-confident.

I began doing the spiritual exercises regularly, and the meditation, as taught in Yogananda's lessons. I had to fulfil my goal, which was self-realisation. I felt strongly that there was something beyond the empty, shallow, material life, something deeper, more meaningful. I was determined to do whatever was necessary to experience it. In one of the books was the following saying of a Maharaj: "*The Self, the Truth, the Reality, cannot be found outside oneself; it comes from within, and has to be experienced. It can only be experienced through meditation. It is in peace and silence that you grow.*" Yogananda also stated: "*Those who search sincerely would surely be led to God or Guru at the right Time*". It was now the right time for me.

However, before I was able to pursue my longing for spiritual enlightenment, there came a development in my marriage, which justified all my sister's fears. I now came face to face with a different and deeply hurtful type of reality.

Chapter 7

THE END OF A MARRIAGE

The heart of a man has to be toughened, not hardened, and only blows of loss, grief and distress can achieve this.

Sathya Sai Baba

It would take too long to write about all the painful details that brought about the final break-up of my forty years of marriage. I will simply mention a few major incidents, which led to it, though they subsequently turned out to be yet again stepping stones and guidance on my spiritual journey.

Many men are victims of their ego. Unfortunately for them, they do not learn from the painful experiences of so many rich and famous men, and some rich but not famous men who fall for younger women whose sole motive is to feather their own nests. These women are lured by the security, status and glamour of a life of affluence, which they can gain through flattering and nurturing the older man's ego. They make them feel that they are still young, attractive and desirable, and the men fall blindly into the trap, wanting to recapture a few more years of youth and excitement, but at what a cost!

They do not realise that these women are scheming, cold and calculating, with no true love in their hearts. They will rarely sit and nurse or care for them once the money or health has disappeared. These men find out only too late (as happened in my case), that the wives, who were with them, supporting and encouraging them when they were building their future together, would be the ones who would be by their side through thick and thin, if and when things went wrong. These men look back too late, and realise that they have lost the one woman who had been at their side when they had nothing, sharing all the ups and downs until success had been achieved. The short-lived adventure and excitement turns into bitter realisation of their foolishness. To be wise is to learn from other's painful mistakes, and not to follow the same path, which causes much pain, and at great loss!

A few months before our daughter Diana married Harry, at the end of 1977, I engaged a new 'au pair' (whom I previously mentioned) to help me with the housework and baby-sit for my son Robin who was seven years old at the time. Despite my initial, instinctive misgivings, she persuaded me to take her on, and give her a chance.

The au pair was half French, half Vietnamese and was born in Vietnam. She worked well, did everything to please me and soon won my trust and affection. I treated her like a daughter. She got on very well with our son Robin, and this naturally pleased us.

However, after some months, I noticed the extra attention she was showing to my husband, but she said she considered us like her parents, and that my husband reminded her of her father. Despite her words, as time went on, I began to feel that there was something insincere, even antagonistic, about her.

Once at her request I was giving her Healing. I normally do this with closed eyes. When, momentarily, I opened my eyes I was taken aback at the way she looked at me, a strange and unkindly look, contemptuous, arrogant and belittling. I was shocked. With hindsight I have since realised these antagonistic vibrations emanating from her, to have been her unkindly thoughts directed towards me. I felt her envy and jealousy. I tried to dismiss from my mind the bad impressions, which I was getting, wanting to believe that I was mistaken.

The au pair finally completed her year's stay with us and returned to France. Three months later I received a telephone call from her mother who asked me whether my husband and I would agree to her daughter coming back to England to work in my husband's business, as she had completed a short secretarial course but was too nervous to work in France. She said that apparently the bosses in France were very strict and demanding and difficult to work for. Her daughter therefore needed some work experience to gain confidence before she could take a job in France. Her mother assured me that it would only be for a two or three month period. I must say, I was taken aback by this unexpected request, but I was naïve enough to believe her and was completely unsuspecting of the scheming behind it.

It was agreed between my husband and myself that the au pair was going to find herself lodgings nearby and not come back into our home. But when she arrived she said that she was nervous to live by herself and would give me a hand with the housework. I still had no real suspicion at the time, just an uneasy feeling toward her and although I did not feel happy about it, I felt that since it would only be for a three-month period, I agreed.

The three months of her stay as secretary had passed, and she seemed to be deeply involved in my husband's business. She showed no signs of going home. I began to notice here and there incidents, which made me feel uneasy. When I asked my husband when she was going back to France, he said that she was a great help in the office especially at this crucial time. The business was in difficulty and her knowledge of French and English was essential till he could build up his business on the Continent. He therefore needed her to stay on a while longer.

My husband was by now well aware and resigned to the fact that I pursued my interest in Yoga and that I was following the spiritual path of The Self Realisation Fellowship. I had mentioned to him the retreat and convocation. Some while later I was taken aback with shock and surprise when he uttered the following words. "I think the Self Realization Fellowship had done you a lot of good, if you want to go there I will arrange your flight!

I was, I remember, in two minds whether to go and leave my husband with the au pair/secretary alone at home. But I quickly dismissed my inner hunch and put my suspicions aside. I felt a great need to be in a spiritual environment, and here was my chance, which I felt unable to miss. So I accepted the offer and took the risk, although in my heart of hearts I had doubts about their relationship. I still did not want to believe in this possibility. Thus I chose my spiritual need, as my quest for God was stronger than my fear of the risk I was taking by going.

When I arrived home from this latest trip, I began to notice that there was visibly a bond between them, which appeared, more than was appropriate. I had a strange feeling as if I was an outsider in my own home. She had become assertive in her views and generally behaving with self-confidence as if she was the lady of the house. The fact that she was constantly with my husband, going to work with him in the morning and coming back with him in the evening, brought them closer together and this no doubt boosted that self-confidence. She seemed more in control of my husband, and was forceful in her views and opinions. She began to criticise my daughters, especially Diana who was the apple of her father's eye. There were many more incidents, which had disturbed and upset me and served to further increase my suspicions.

This young woman happened to come into our home just a few months before Diana was married to Harry and left for Hong Kong. With Diana away there arose a gap in my husband's life. He now missed the interest he shared with Diana and her show-jumping events. He was at a loss at that point and vulnerable, which the au pair realised only too well and took full advantage of the situation. My husband felt flattered by the interest she was showing in him, and before he realised how far the situation would take him, he was falling into the trap and was now on the road of no return.

At that point I began to be more and more convinced that there was an affair going on between them. My husband's attitude and behaviour towards me changed dramatically. He became distant and cold in the way he spoke to me. For the first time in our married life he was no longer calling me 'darling' or 'cherie' – it was just Ruth when talking to me or calling out to me. He seemed to look at her frequently as if for approval of whatever he said or did.

It was plain to see what was going on, yet something inside me feared to admit to myself the reality of the situation, as a showdown with my husband was something I could not face. He was a strong-willed man, always persuasive and winning arguments, capable of making up things and sounding totally convincing, making me feel that I was being unreasonable and emotional and that I was imagining things which had no foundation. No wonder he was a brilliant salesman who became a self-made millionaire through this gift. He could literally sell ice to the Eskimos or sand to the Bedouins!

The atmosphere in the house became heavy and uncomfortable, as I insisted she had to go. When my husband realised that I was now seriously suspicious of their relationship, he came up with a new idea, telling me that he decided to open a branch in Brussels, that she could run the office there as she was fluent in French and already knew the business. I was unhappy as to this turn of events.

They must have planned the Belgian business venture for some time between them. Nevertheless, she still needed my consent to it since I was a 49% shareholder in the company. The next day she came to me pleading that I should allow her to help my husband set up his office in Brussels and promising that as soon as things started working out she would leave and return home to her family. I finally and reluctantly agreed as I felt that if I went against this plan I would be blamed and bear the responsibility for the financial difficulties we would find ourselves in, or so my husband wanted me to believe.

They left for Brussels and I was not given the hotel details where they were staying. I had to find this out for myself by telephoning the office. A call to the Brussels hotel revealed the reason for my husband omitting to give me the relevant information.

When I phoned and asked the hotel reception if I could speak to Mr. Grant the receptionist replied, "Mr. and Mrs. Grant have just left!" Needless to say, I was beside myself with rage. It confirmed without a doubt what I already knew. It was one thing to suspect but another to be told so plainly the real truth. A close friend who was with me at that time heard the conversation and said to me that she was not surprised, as she and her husband had suspected it for a long time. It seems everybody knew except me, confirming the saying – "the wife is always the last to know!"

That evening I called the hotel again and managed to speak to my husband. I repeated to him what the hotel receptionist had told me. I could no longer avoid a confrontation. I screamed down the telephone, demanding an end to the affair. I felt that my scream was so loud that I was sure my voice could have been heard in Belgium without the telephone! I then telephoned the au pair's mother in Paris and told her just what I thought of her daughter, the marriage wrecker. She denied it! I remember then how deviously she had asked me to take her daughter back into our home for the so-called 'secretarial experience', after she had already returned to France. It seemed she needed more time to be with my husband to finish the 'job' she had started – to break our marriage in order to feather her own nest.

Following the showdown on the telephone to Belgium, my husband hurried home the next day when again I confronted him. He still tried to deny their obvious affair, but looked guilty and unconvincing. He reassured me saying that he had taken her back to her parents and closed the office in Belgium. He convinced me that this was the end of the affair.

His travels to Europe were frequent. This he said was because he was engaged in keeping contacts with different firms for his future business. He often drove himself on these trips, which enabled him to enjoy the full power of his sports car. The day after he left on one of his trips, I received a telephone call from him from a clinic in Paris saying he needed an emergency operation for his haemorrhoids, which had suddenly started to bleed badly causing him to collapse upon his arrival in Paris.

He explained to me that he had felt so ill that he had no choice but to call the au pair's family to come to his aid. She took him to a private clinic, where it was suggested that they needed to operate on him urgently. When he telephoned me from the clinic there was great anxiety in his voice. He was crying, saying that they required my consent for the operation. He was obviously very frightened. I said that I must first consult with our own GP before allowing them to go ahead.

I contacted my GP who suggested that we should bring my husband back home and assured me that the small delay in dealing with it would not endanger his life. I telephoned the clinic in Paris and instructed them to send my husband to the airport in an ambulance, as I wanted him to be treated at home.

He arrived at Heathrow Airport, where I had an ambulance waiting to take him to a London hospital, with me following behind in my car. When he was examined, the specialist who attended him discovered a serious deep-seated pelvic infection which could have cost him his life had he been operated on in France in that condition. They had obviously either not diagnosed the infection or did not weigh the danger of the operation without first treating the infection. The specialist who treated my husband mentioned to me that if they had operated on him in Paris, he would have most probably died as the infection would have spread and poisoned him. My bringing him home saved his life.

Some months later, he advised me that he was moving his business from London and going into a new partnership in Birmingham. I had no reason to be suspicious as he convinced me he was living in his partner's home during his stay in Birmingham. The partner had a large house and they were happy to have my husband staying with them. He instructed me not to telephone their home, as it would disturb them. Instead he had a mobile telephone and told me to call him on that line or at the factory, which he had set up with his partner.

Soon after, my husband's health started to deteriorate. He suffered a mild heart attack, which resulted in heart bypass surgery. He came out of hospital and stayed home only for about a week, whereas he should have stayed at least one or two months to recover from the operation, but he seemed in a great hurry to return to Birmingham.

Since he had moved to Birmingham, my husband was constantly telling me that he could not afford to keep our home with the heated swimming pool. The upkeep was too much just for Robin and me as he was away all week. My husband asked me to look for a smaller house during the week, and when he came at the weekend, he would view it. While we were viewing some houses which I listed, I had a strange feeling from the way my husband was looking at the property and discussing our move that he was arranging everything for Robin and myself, not as if he was going to be there with us. This puzzled me, but as I could not find an explanation for it, I dismissed it from my thoughts.

In January 1984 I discovered a small lump under my ear lobe. It was a tumour and needed an immediate operation to prevent it becoming cancerous. I went to hospital, all on my own. My husband never came from Birmingham to be with me.

On the day I arrived home from hospital, I had a visit from my cousin Alice, her daughter Roberta, and her husband Martin, who expressed surprise at the absence of my husband. They suggested that I should go to Birmingham to see what was going on there. From their looks, they appeared to insinuate that my husband might be having an affair. I dismissed their suspicions, saying that he was too concerned and involved in re-building his business now and had neither time nor the money to have an affair.

Soon after they left, a friend arrived. Whilst my friend was with me I received a telephone call from my husband's business partner asking to speak to him. I said that I had not seen my husband and that I had just come out of hospital after an operation, on a benign lump under my earlobe.

I said I thought my husband was in Birmingham with him. At that moment something clicked in my mind and I heard myself say to him "Is there anything going on in Birmingham that I should know about?" A pregnant pause at the other end of the line made my pulse race. His voice came back asking, "Do you really want to know?" I said, "Yes, please tell me everything".

He then revealed that my husband had brought the au pair and their two-year-old daughter over from France and that they were living in a new house, which my husband had bought in a nice suburb of Birmingham.

He also told me that the au pair was coming to the factory interfering in the business, and asking the staff to call her Mrs. Grant. As he put the telephone down, my heart was racing and thumping so strongly that I could hear its beat. I put my hand over my heart as it felt as though it would jump right out of my chest.

My friend who was sitting next to me realised that I had received some bad news. She looked at me with concern. I told her what I had just heard. She took valium from her purse and told me to take it to calm me down.

As soon as I regained control of myself, I telephoned my eldest daughter, Diana, who according to my husband's business partner, had known about the affair for some time. I informed her that I knew all that was going on with her father. She was silent for a second. I suppose she was a bit shocked to hear me speak calmly about it, probably expecting me to be hysterical. Instead I told her to make an immediate appointment with a solicitor whose name I had once given her.

The solicitor acted speedily and obtained a court order freezing the proceeds of the sale of our house, which had just been completed, preventing any money being paid to my husband. An injunction was also obtained preventing disposal of all his assets.

I could not believe that the loving husband, who had looked after me and cared for me since I was seventeen years old, was the one I could not trust anymore and I would now have to fight him to secure my future, and that of my son. I felt cheated and humiliated.

From the moment I found out about his double life in Birmingham, the shock and trauma of this discovery stopped me from looking for a house and therefore from making arrangements to remove all the contents of our large family home, much of which would have had to be sold or disposed of, as we were going to move into a smaller house. I was given only a week in which to make all the necessary arrangements and organise the move. This situation struck me like a bombshell and I was paralysed mentally, and unable to deal with the move. Meanwhile the week I was given had elapsed. I explained my situation to the developers and they agreed to give me an extension for one more week to remove all our belongings.

The developers bought our house with the plan to demolish it in order to build an estate on our large plot as well as on the six-acre allotment behind our house. Everything therefore had to be sold, disposed of, What was left would be taken by the demolishers, or it would go under the bulldozer.

I wanted to sell the valuable items to convert them into cash rather than see everything go under the bulldozer or leave it for the demolition contractors. I placed an advertisement in the local paper for all the fixtures and fittings, which were of special high quality. Our Italian marble fireplace, pine ceiling beams, carved mahogany banisters, top quality kitchen equipment, light fittings, our beautiful bathrooms and gold plated fittings, swimming pool filters, and even the beautiful rose garden and plants, urns etc.

Because the house was of an unusual design, it was very well known in the area and as soon as people heard it was going to be demolished, plants and features in the garden disappeared overnight, obviously stolen. People were coming to view what there was for sale and took full advantage of my circumstances. All my beautiful and expensive fixtures and fittings went for next to nothing. My beautiful banisters were pulled out and taken away. My pine ceiling beams were pulled out. Things were ripped out of the walls, including my beautiful Italian bathroom and all my kitchen equipments. My home of twenty years was being destroyed in front of my eyes.

I was all on my own handling all these people with my elderly mother who came from Israel to be with me. There are no words to describe how I felt. It was as if I was being dismembered bit-by-bit, day-by-day. As each day dawned, I found out that things were stolen; my lovely rose shrubs and plants were dug up leaving holes everywhere in my garden. I was heartbroken. It was so sorrowful for my mother to witness all this. I worried about her and how it would affect her health.

As if all this was not enough, one morning I got a telephone call from my next- door neighbour (I had already moved temporarily to my daughter's house while going daily to my own home to remove the rest of our belongings). The neighbour said that my garage had been broken into and that she saw our furniture, which I had stored there until I could organise a removal firm to collect it, had been taken away.

I rushed over to my house only to find that the demolition people had taken over the house in spite of the fact that I still had two more days left of the extended date. They could not wait to enter the house to take what they could. My beautiful Italian bedroom furniture, as well as the furniture in my son's room, curtains and other items which I had locked in the garage were all gone, as well as my freezer. I was devastated.

When I asked the demolition people where the furniture had gone, they said they knew nothing about the disappearance of my furniture or other items, and warned me rather rudely that I should not touch anything, as the house was theirs now.

I said that I had two more days to finish collecting my belongings but they almost physically threw me out of my house. They would not even let me take out our family films, which were in a box in my son's room. I felt crushed and heartbroken.

While I was staying temporarily at my daughter's home, Kathy, my ex-daily help, came to visit me. She said that at the reception of Diana and Harry's wedding that had been held at our home, she was in the kitchen talking with the au pair. She told her that she thought Harry was far too old for Diana (there was a 21 years age difference). Kathy told me how it shocked her when the au pair replied, "Better ten good years with an old man than a lifetime of struggle with a young man"! I was not surprised to hear that as it confirmed to me that this woman had worked out her plan from the minute she came into our home. The au pair was in fact 36 years younger than my husband.

The battle for a fair settlement between my husband and myself through our solicitors with ever rising costs lasted over two years, which only served to lengthen the pain and my utter bewilderment of how he could possibly put me through all this.

At times I was reflecting how incredibly and appropriately symbolic that my marriage and my home were destroyed simultaneously, including all the family films! There had to be some reason and meaning to all this, but at the time I did not know what or where all this would lead me.

As this trauma ensued, my mind was in turmoil, seeing everything around me literally falling apart. It was as if my life needed to be totally destroyed that I might have to rebuild it from scratch again on solid spiritual foundations (although I did not realise this until years later). At that point I felt that I lost the only person I used to rely on and trust to make all the important decisions in our life. It was impossible for me to take it all in. I felt as if I was sinking into an abyss of complete hopelessness. The husband I had trusted with my life for forty years had betrayed me and abandoned his young son.

In fact, when my husband had asked my father for my hand when I was still barely seventeen, and a minor, he vowed to my father that he would look after me for the rest of my life. My father reluctantly agreed to this arranged marriage, because my mother had already given her consent. My parents had divorced five years earlier with much acrimony and my father wanted to protect me from any further pain.

After our marriage I was to be totally dependant on my husband, especially as I had to leave home and country to follow him to Egypt, the country where he was born and lived, although he was a British subject. It was hard to believe that he was now my adversary and I could trust him no longer. He now had another family to care for and I was in their way. It became a matter of them against me. Now at the age of fifty six I was left with our young son Robin who was only fourteen years old and, at such a vulnerable age, had to come to terms with the fact that his father was no longer there for him. I felt crushed, abandoned, betrayed.

However, out of my state of despair, an inner strength and determination prevented me from giving up this battle of my life. Years before I had had a similar battle after the tragedy of my car accident. I had to fight and overcome this new tragedy, no matter how difficult, not only for my sake but also for that of my son's future. I could not possibly allow this situation to destroy me. I was determined not to give 'her' the satisfaction of stepping into my shoes and achieving her wicked selfish plan. I would fight to the end, I knew that if I lost it would mean that I would have to go to them with a begging bowl for my financial support and I would rather have died than let that happen. Because of the extremely high costs of our solicitors, my husband telephoned to me and said that he would agree to a reasonable settlement, and that to save high costs, we should use a family friend as our solicitor to draw up the final settlement. I agreed, as I knew that the injunction was protecting my interests.

From time to time I telephoned one of the employees who worked at the factory in Birmingham, who was very sympathetic to my situation, to ask what was going on, just to keep a check on things. On this occasion she mentioned to me that some people came to look at the machines with a view to buying. I was shocked, as I knew that the injunction was still on and therefore it would not have been possible for my husband to dispose of any assets.

I immediately telephoned our 'friend' and solicitor to alert him of this fact but was told by his partner that he was in

Scotland on business. I told the partner what was happening in the factory and instructed him to take a court order at once against my husband. He said that he would do it immediately.

In spite of his promise, I drove immediately to his office to personally confirm this instruction. A short while after returning home from the solicitor's office there was a knock on the door and a courier handed me a file. When I opened and read the first few pages, I discovered to my horror that the injunction had already been lifted!

Within about five minutes the courier returned asking for the file back, which he said he had delivered to me in error. I sent him away and kept the file. It was obvious that this file had not been despatched to the court as I had requested. It seemed that the partner had not even looked at the files and was not aware that the injunction had been lifted already, my solicitor obviously had not told him. But by 'Divine intervention' the file was delivered to me by 'mistake' so as to alert me to what was taking place behind my back and quite contrary to my instructions.

I sat frozen with shock for a few minutes. I then telephoned the solicitor's office speaking again with the partner telling him of my discovery. He told me to come to the office the next day, as my solicitor would be back from Scotland by then.

I arrived at the office at 9.00 a.m. the next morning and saw the solicitor. I showed him the file and the letter, which stated that the injunction had been lifted. He seemed uneasy and shocked when I confronted him with this. Not knowing what to reply he simply said that his partner must have done it in his absence 'in error'!

I immediately knew that he had betrayed me, leaving my interests totally unprotected. I would now have to accept whatever my husband wished to settle for. I lost the lever I had over him for which I paid a considerable amount of money to the first solicitor.

I told this 'friend' how shocked and devastated I was that he had let me down. He muttered some apology; I took no notice and walked out. Within three days I received his bill for £6,000, which he had already deducted and paid to himself from my account at the building society. He had taken over my case only just under a month before to draft the final settlement with my husband. I realised from a few discussions that I had with him that he had not even bothered to look at my file or know the details of my case. He ruined all that I had hoped to achieve, betraying my trust in him.

I had no doubt in my mind that my husband, having failed to pressurise me to lift the injunction, must have somehow 'persuaded' the solicitor to do this without my knowledge. It was a stab in the back. I was told that I could take this second solicitor to court over this and he would be struck off for his professional misconduct, but I just could not handle yet another battle on my own with all the emotional and financial consequences.

I had yet again to find a third lawyer to complete the settlement. I managed to find one who was at least sympathetic and honest. I also found out to my dismay that my husband had removed my son and myself from the private medical insurance with BUPA, replacing us with his new family.

This was another blow, which I had to come to terms with. Furthermore, the weekly maintenance which had been paid to me through the court order arranged by the first solicitor, had now stopped as well. How much more could I take?

But the fight was on and I had to deal with every situation – swim or sink. After months of negotiation through my third solicitor, we finally reached a settlement, which I had no choice but to accept. Within a short while I heard that my husband had sold all the machines and assets of the factory. One machine was transferred on the au pair's name to a factory in France on rental. They packed everything up and moved to Spain.

Out of the rubble of my broken marriage, home, and life, surprisingly, far from breaking down I emerged stronger, more determined, confident and independent. That did not happen immediately. The road was long, painful, rough, with twists and turns, with seemingly insurmountable obstacles. At times I did not think I could carry on, but as soon as I weakened and felt that I was going to succumb, I turned to God, and my ceaseless prayers were always heard and answered. Ultimately, a number of years later, peace and contentment beyond my dreams were to come into my life when I discovered the Universal Spiritual Teacher and Avatar, Sri Sathya Sai Baba.

I had been sorely tested, by an accident, divorce, betrayals, disaster upon disaster, but my spirit, my resolve, had been sharpened, and my faith strengthened, especially as I learned more and more about the remarkable and inspiring teacher in India.

Picture No 1: My cousin Helen, my sister Miki, and myself with the crossover my head

मेरे साई
प्यारे साई

Picture No. 4: The Hospital in Puttaparthi.

Picture No. 5: Nine Large Jars Completely Filled With Vibuthi.

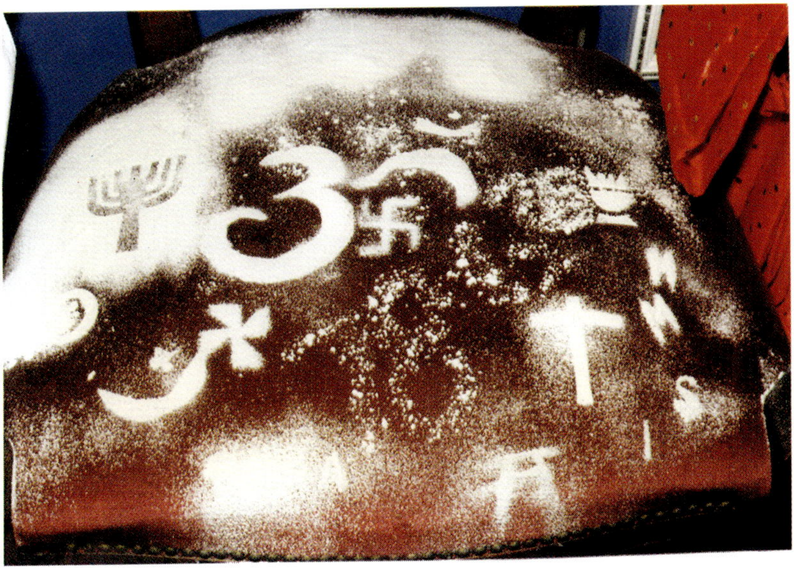

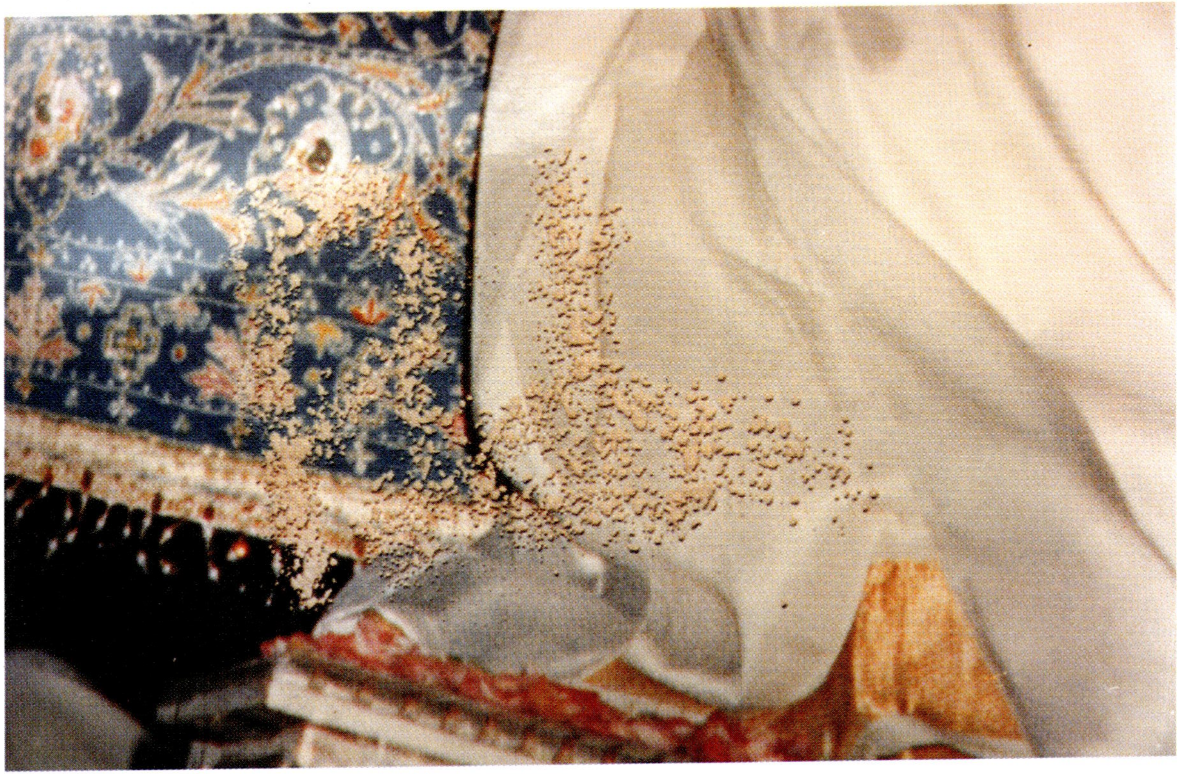

Picture No. 8: Photograph signed "Baba" with vibhuthi

Picture No. 9: With Love Written in Orange Sandalwood paint on Baba's Picture.

Picture No 10: The Picture of Baba from Mr Patel's Temple

Picture No.11: The Gold Ring Manifested for me by Baba

Picture 12: The Coconut

PART TWO

INTRODUCTION

I have separated the account of my life at this point since the whole emphasis changes. An old world of trouble and constant stress lay behind me and a new hope, indeed a new world, emerged.

There is no doubt I had always been searching, seeking, for truth, for understanding. This had taken me twice to the retreat of Yogananda in America. But again and again all the demands of daily life, home, children, drew me back along the paths of duty to those close to me.

However, once the split from my husband was final, I was able to renew my search. Possibly the materialism in which he was deeply embedded impelled me further away from his world into the world of the spirit.

And so, almost as if planned, I came across a remarkable Master, who has been a great inspiration to me, and whose teachings and radiant personality changed my life. This part of my story therefore revolves around my discovery of Sri Sathya Sai Baba, the Teacher from Puttaparthi, in India.

Chapter 8

FIRST STEPS TO BABA

Have constructive thoughts,
Consoling words,
Compassionate acts.
The wise are those who know the Self

Sathya Sai Baba

After all that had happened to me it is difficult to describe my state of mind and the emotional turmoil I was left in. Whenever I felt overcome by events that had crushed me to the ground, the only escape I found was to lie down on my settee, with the curtains closed, and fall asleep, blotting out for a short while the trauma of my shattered life. It was unbelievable how quickly and peacefully I would fall asleep, as if someone had waved a magic wand over me and gave me a beautiful, peaceful rest so that I felt recharged when I awoke.

I tried painfully to put the shattered pieces of my life together. My forty-year long marriage had broken down. At the age of 56 I had thought that we were settled into our lives, with three children and four grandchildren. We had all one could wish for, materially. We were enjoying the fruits of labour of many years, but fate obviously had other plans.

Because of the devastating shock when the bombshell of my husband's affair and his illegitimate child fell upon me, and the mental pain and the stress of it all, it was no wonder that one day when I was at the hairdresser she told me that there was a small bald patch at the back of my head. I thought nothing of it, as I believed that the hair would just grow back. However, gradually, over some months, another patch appeared, and a little while later I began to notice a few little patches here and there on my scalp.

My doctor sent me to a dermatologist, who told me I had a certain type of Alopecia. The steroids she advocated only increased the baldness. Looking at it, my heart sank. Another specialist advised that there was no cure for this condition and that I would lose all of my hair within a few years. A further specialist confirmed the previous prognosis.

What could I do, who could I turn to? I only have God. He is my father and mother. I would turn to Him and accept whatever was to be. On arriving home after visiting the specialist I parked my car in the driveway and sat, frozen with despair, on my seat. I could not get out. I leaned over the steering wheel and broke down in a flood of tears.

Suddenly I heard a knock on my car window. It was my next-door neighbour, Parina. She had come out to put some rubbish in the bin and had seen me bent over the wheel. I rolled down my window. She asked if I was all right. I told her all that the doctor had said. She then told me that she knew of a Chinese herbalist doctor in Soho who apparently cured a child of a colleague of hers of a serious and extreme case of eczema and asthma. She also told me that this doctor had been very successful in curing many types of skin problems. I asked her for the address and she promised to give it to me.

Meanwhile, I had made up my mind that I would on no account have the treatment with steroids. If my eventual baldness was unavoidable I would rather lose my hair but be otherwise healthy. I would not risk suffering the serious side effects of this treatment. If the worst happened I could always wear a wig and get on with my life, rather than spending the rest of my days in and out of hospital with added problems.

In the meantime I would try every alternative treatment available and this I did. I tried every avenue, followed so many different treatments over a six-year period that it would take too long to describe. The main one was the Chinese herbalist in Soho, London. Her clinic operated then on a system of first come, first served. I got up the next morning at 4.00 a.m., arriving at her surgery at 4.30 a.m. There were already four people waiting there, one lady having come all the way from Manchester and apparently slept most of the night on the doorstep of the clinic with her three year-old daughter!

When my turn came I went into the room to see the doctor, I was greeted with a lovely, warm, friendly smile. This lady doctor immediately won my trust. She gave me some herbal lotion to rub over my scalp as well as herbal tablets. The herbs were very expensive - £70 for one month's supply. I thought I would give it a try. I kept going to the herbalist once a month for her to check on the result and get a fresh supply of remedies.

Three weeks later, my neighbour Parina came to tell me about a holy man she knew in Finchley, London, who she thought might be able to help. She said that her mother, sister and many other people she knew went to him for all sorts of problems, that he blessed them and they found him to be of great help. I had nothing to lose and said I would go whenever she was ready. We decided to go the following evening, which was in March 1991.

We knocked and a tall, kindly-looking Indian man, who I estimated, to be in his sixties, (I later found out that he was 75!) opened the door. I was surprised to see hanging on the wall a photograph of my guru, Paramahansa Yogananda, amongst portraits of other holy men. We entered the temple room where the walls were covered by pictures of many Indian Deities. The room was filled with the aroma of incense. Apart from the utensils used for 'Puja' (Indian worship ritual), there were coconuts, Kum Kum (red powder), rice, nuts, sweets which were given as prasad (blessed food).

Parina told him about my problems. He summoned me to come and sit in front of him. He prayed and blessed me and assured me that all would be well. I felt peaceful and hopeful.

When we came out of his flat, Parina asked me whether I heard what he had said to me when he showed us in. I said that I had paid no attention as I thought he was addressing her, since he did not know me. She told me that he had greeted me with the words 'Sai Ram' I asked her why he would say that to me (I remembered vaguely that 'Sai Ram' was a greeting used by Sai Baba devotees). She told me that she did not know the reason and that he had never greeted her or her family in that way. I was puzzled by these words, so was Parina.

I believe that there is always a reason and a purpose for what happens to us. It is a matter of waiting for the right time for things to be revealed, and the right time came two weeks later. Parina came to me saying that her aunt had taken her to a Sai Baba Temple close to my house, and described what had happened there. She said that she had knelt down to pray and when she got up to go, Mr. Patel's son (in whose home the Temple was) said to her that she could choose one photograph of Sai Baba out of a small pile, and that some of them were blessed with vibhuti (holy ash materialised by Sai Baba) and some were not.

When Parina picked up one of the photographs she looked to see if it was blessed, but it was not. Standing by the door about to go out, Parina's aunt noticed that vibhuti had suddenly appeared on the photograph Parina was holding. Parina said that she was frightened and bewildered, not expecting this to happen to her. After her photograph had been blessed, many good things began to happen in her life. For example, at that particular period, Parina's husband had gone abroad to try to find a job as he was unemployed for quite a long while. During the absence of her husband Parina went to live with her in-laws and put her house for rent with an agent. For some months no one came to look at the house. Suddenly two gentlemen arrived and as soon as they entered the front door they did not even want to look around the house, which surprised her. They said, "Here is three month's deposit in advance, we want the house as from today!"

She was so happy; she could not believe her luck. She cried with happiness and relief to have her house finally let.

Following this, in gratitude, Parina who had become a Baba devotee, decided to fast every Thursday, which is the day they honour their Guru. However, she did not have a photograph of Baba to put on the altar. Nevertheless, she lit a candle and incense stick, then opened the drawer for something, when, to her great surprise, she saw a small photo of Sai Baba right in front of her. She placed it on her altar and said her prayers. Later, on her way to work, she began to wonder how the photograph came to be in her drawer. She remembered clearly that she had recently cleaned and tidied up the drawer and never saw the photograph there.

A few weeks later when her mother-in-law returned from India, Parina asked her whether she had a picture of Sai Baba in the house as she was living with her mother-in law then, but her mother-in-law said that they never had one since they were not followers of Baba. The photograph had been materialised for her by Baba as she so much wished to have it for her prayers!

After an absence of nearly 2 years Parina's husband, Ashwin, returned and they moved back into their home, which they had previously let. Almost immediately upon his return he found a good job.

They had been married for nine years, but Parina had been unable to conceive. They desperately wanted a child and had seen several doctors. She had even been put on hormone treatment but to no avail. A short while after they moved back into their home, Parina had placed a full length photograph of Baba in her sitting room. Incredibly, within a couple of months she conceived and had a beautiful baby girl. Since then, her faith in Sai Baba strengthened by leaps and bounds. A second daughter was born on 1st July 1996, four years after the first child. Needless to say their happiness was complete.

After relating her experiences with Sai Baba, Parina asked if I wished to go with her to Mr. Patel's Temple. We went on the following day, in April 1991. Mr. Patel opened the door and welcomed us. I saw many photographs of Sai Baba as well as other Hindu deities displayed on the walls, most of them blessed with vibhuti (Picture 2). The vibhuti that appears at Mr Patel's Temple has a delicate floral fragrance with a soft powdery texture. There were beautiful flowers adorning the Temple. The atmosphere was one of reverence and tranquillity.

This holy ash is materialised by Sai Baba. It has healing properties and is unique. It is a blessed remedy that no money can buy. Its potent healing power has cured countless pains and diseases. It symbolises the fact that ultimately every material thing perishes, and the only true Reality is our imperishable soul.

One can never tell the effect of vibhuti. Here is an incident where it proved very effective in a case involving an animal. My friend Brenda had three cats, one of which was an albino. This cat, due to too much exposure to the sun, had developed skin cancer on her left ear. After many visits to the vet and much expense, the condition worsened. The vet advised that the only solution to prevent the cancer spreading was to cut off most of the poor cat's ear.

Brenda was very upset, as she adored her cats. She discussed it with her husband before making a decision. She then remembered the packet of vibhuti she had and applied it to the cat's ear for a week or two. To her amazement and joy the condition improved and then miraculously disappeared altogether. The hair even grew back where it was bald due to the cancer!

She showed the cat to the vet to have the cure confirmed. On examining the cat the vet was lost for words, quite stunned. He asked her what she had done. Brenda told him about the miracle remedy of the vibhuti manifested by Sai Baba. The vet asked, "Could you bring me a few packets of this 'stuff'? I could do with it here!" Two years later the cat continued to enjoy perfect health.

All that I had heard from Mr. Patel was truly incredible. Although difficult to accept, I felt Mr. Patel was an honest and humble man. He himself was surprised and in awe that all this should happen in his house, but he accepted that, for some reason, he had been chosen as an instrument through whom people would see and learn of the message of love and selfless service of Sai Baba. His family house became a Temple where people come to pray and find peace in the holy vibrations that are strongly felt there. Yet how did this house become a Temple of prayer and healing?

In May 1988, Mr. and Mrs. Patel decided to build an extension to their house for a snooker room. Little did they know then that this snooker room would become a place of worship. In keeping with tradition there was to be a blessing ceremony in the extension. Photos of Deities were placed around, adorned with garlands of flowers. One of Mr. Patel's friends had brought a photo of Sathya Sai Baba, who is considered to be a Divine incarnation. As part of the ceremony, five coconuts were placed in front of the photos.

After the ceremony all five coconuts had unaccountably split in a straight line across the middle with coconut milk trickling out of them. One kept trickling for a week continuously, which was more milk than a coconut could ever have contained. Another coconut, which had been cut open, was found to have an imprint of Sai Baba's head on the flesh inside the coconut. It was all mind-boggling.

To Mr. Patel's further astonishment, almost all photographs were covered with sweet-scented ash, which seemed to be growing out of them. At the time Mr. Patel knew nothing about Sai Baba or vibhuti. When this ash began to materialise, Mr. Patel was told that his home had been blessed by the grace of Sai Baba. He was asked by the priest to leave it for a 'few days' for devotees and people to come and see it. Mr. Patel thought that within a few days all would be over and he would be able to set up the snooker table for his sons.

This however was not to be. As news of the miracles spread people streamed, sometimes in coach loads, into the house. The 'few days' turned into weeks, the weeks into months, the months into years. Needless to say, the snooker table had to be sold! Meanwhile, more manifestations took place. Mr. Patel was by now convinced that he had to keep the place as a Temple for people to come, see and share in these phenomena and blessings. This seems to be Baba's way of awakening and alerting people to the spiritual dimension of which many or most are unaware. Baba had taken up His mission when barely fourteen years of age. Discarding his school books, He declared: "I have come to reconstruct the ancient highway to God. My task is the spiritual regeneration of humanity through truth and love".

Mr. Patel told me that none of his family had believed in Baba or knew much about Him before all this happened. After witnessing the 'strange' appearance of vibhuti and other phenomena, he became convinced of Baba's divine powers and omnipresence. The Temple was open to people of all religions (or none), since Baba embraces all religions as One.

On all the walls of the Temple were photographs of many Hindu Deities, and Saints of different faiths, including Hinduism, Christianity, Sikhism, Islam, Judaism, Zoroasterism, and Buddhism. Each person would find his or her faith represented in this beautiful Temple. Baba says "God is only One, although people see Him in different forms and call Him by different names. Therefore, you should worship God in the name and form familiar to you". Unlike most other places of worship, Mr. Patel is totally against anyone leaving any money in the Temple. In fact he has put the following message for all to see: *"Please do not leave your money here, only leave your anger, ego, bad thoughts and rudeness. Love all, serve all". Sai Baba.*

When I was with Parina at Mr. Patel's house she suggested I should leave a letter there as she had done when she had the problem of renting her house, a problem that was resolved almost immediately. Her aunt's problems also cleared up after she left a letter at the Temple. I thought I had nothing to lose by doing likewise, so I wrote down a few lines about my problems and concerns, placing it in a box which was full of letters. Perhaps I would get a response in some form.

Mr. Patel asked me what I did with my spare time. I told him I was retired but had been busily involved as a member of the fund-raising committee of the NSPCC (National Society for Prevention of Cruelty to Children) for fifteen years. I mentioned I was also doing healing in the local church hall in Harrow. He asked whether I would be willing to do healing in his Temple, as many people were in need of it. I was surprised at his request and touched that he should ask me to help in this way. I immediately agreed indicating that it would be a privilege to be a channel for healing in such a holy place.

I left Mr. Patel's house feeling great peace and upliftment. When I arrived home I felt as if I had been cleansed from within and that all the stress and tension that I had experienced since the break-up of my marriage had just vanished. A few days later I received from my solicitor the divorce papers that I signed without any hesitation. Strangely, I felt totally detached and liberated as if the umbilical cord had been finally cut. I felt free. Before this I just could not let go of the marriage and was unable even to look at or sign the divorce papers for years.

On the following Friday I went to Mr. Patel's Temple. After the Bhajan (singing) was over, five or six people were waiting to receive healing. I only saw two of them as it was getting late. I told the others still waiting that I would see them at another arranged time. I suggested to Mr. Patel that Sunday afternoon would be a convenient time for people to come. I told him I would contact friends of mine, a married couple, who were healers and also devotees of Sai Baba to join me since it would be impossible for me alone to attend to all the people who sought healing.

Later on I contacted my friends, Dulcie and Desmond, who had just returned from their first visit to Sai Baba's ashram in India. Since their return they had begun healing in their own home. I felt that they would be the right people to join me. They were very pleased I had asked them to help and agreed to meet me at the Temple on the following Sunday.

From 1.30 p.m. on Sunday we were kept busy with patients all afternoon. Every Sunday afternoon Mr. Patel's home was turned into a hospital ward. People came in wheelchairs and on crutches, with all manner of ailments on which doctors had either given up or for which conventional treatments were of little help.

After a month I remembered the letter I had placed in a box full of many other letters. When the healing was over I went to look for my letter, but could not find it. As I was about to give up, Mr. Patel's ten year old nephew Bhavish, walked in and offered to help me. I told him that he would not know my handwriting and with so many letters it would be a waste of time to continue looking for it. However he insisted, saying, "I will find it". So I suggested that we should make a short prayer to Baba to help us. I must admit I did not think we would find it, as there were a few boxes with so many letters. However, I had barely finished my prayer when Bhavish put his hand into the pile of letters, pulling one out at random. He showed it to me, saying, "Is this your letter?" It was. How can I describe my utter amazement, wonder and excitement?

I hurried to Mr. Patel who was in the adjoining room, saying excitedly that his nephew had found my letter! I tried to open the envelope and made a little tear at the corner, but it was tightly sealed and I did not want to damage the envelope. I handed it to Mr. Patel. He held and felt it with his fingers, saying, "I feel there is vibhuti in the letter". I could not believe it. I asked for a knife to open the envelope. I pulled out the letter carefully as it was folded several times. I unfolded it, and, lo and behold, inside the folds my letter was covered with vibhuti! I literally jumped for joy and cried with delight. I could not believe my eyes, but there it was, vibhuti had actually appeared inside my sealed envelope. What a blessing! I treasure the letter to this day.

Since coming to Mr. Patel's Temple I have had the privilege of witnessing many such manifestations. One that happens often is when Baba leaves religious signs and symbols, in vibhuti on 'His' chair. In 1993 He started putting signs of all the world's religions on the one chair, starting with OM (the primordial sound of creation) in the middle and then other signs appeared around it for a week (Picture 3).

Mr. Patel covered the whole chair with Perspex to preserve and protect these holy symbols. Baba had obviously not finished His message as He then put the first letter from the word of each of the five human values (Sathya *(Truth)*, Dharma *(Right Conduct)*, Prema *(Love)*, Shanti *(Peace)*, Ahimsa *(Non-violence)*,) beneath the chair, after it had been sealed with Perspex for protection. On His footstool He put the word love, and another big OM sign appeared under the chair. Sometime later, another OM appeared in orange coloured vibhuti on top of the Perspex

In Mrs. Patel's kitchen, empty jars were suddenly filled to the brim with vibhuti, which was used for healing at the Temple (Picture 5). Amazingly, each time the jars were depleted, they would be filled up again. Each patient also received a packet of vibhuti after the healing to use by adding some in a little water to drink and also to apply to any affected area. We were happy to witness many wonderful healing results.

The numbers of people coming increased week by week. Mr. Patel's home was too small to contain such numbers. His neighbours had complained about the traffic and cars parked outside their homes. A doctor friend of Mr. Patel heard about the problem and offered the use of his surgery on a Sunday afternoon, as it was not then being used. There was a forecourt for cars and enough room for healing and a large waiting room.

Our healing work at the Temple lasted for three years. The suggestion of the surgery was a godsend and the time was just right! We moved to the surgery the following Sunday, leaving the beautiful vibrations and atmosphere of the Temple with regret. We mentioned this to Mr. Patel who quickly reassured us that Baba's grace and blessing would be with us at the surgery as well.

In order to create a spiritual atmosphere in the surgery, we prepared a small altar in the kitchen with Baba's photograph and flowers near His picture. I went to attend to my first patient. When I finished I had to go through the kitchen to the bathroom to wash my hands (after each healing hands were always washed). On returning through the kitchen where the altar was, I saw large blobs of vibhuti had appeared on Baba's photograph! This vibhuti had not been there previously. It was a photograph I had brought from my home and placed in the kitchen myself. As I looked at it I suddenly felt an overwhelming feeling of love that moved me to tears.

I went to tell Dulcie and Desmond but they were healing in their separate rooms so I pulled my next patient by the hand into the kitchen to show her what Baba had just done. She looked at the picture, and went on her knees in reverence.

This wonderful yet unexpected manifestation had moved me so deeply, that while I was giving healing, I could not control the tears of joy which streamed down my face. I felt strongly that there was a holy Presence in the room. That outpouring of love I felt continued throughout the healing. Afterwards the lady to whom I gave healing told me that she too was moved by the whole experience. It gave her a feeling of peace and upliftment. Meanwhile, Dulcie, Desmond and Ivan, another healer who had joined us, had gone into the kitchen and seen what had happened. They were ecstatic to realise that Baba had blessed our new venue and would be with us as he had been in the Temple.

Meanwhile something quite unexpected happened to me at Mr. Patel's Temple, which brought me closer to Sai Baba.

On Sunday of 14th July 1991, which happened to be my birthday, the following incident happened. Just a few days previously, Wednesday 10th July, a dear friend telephoned me asking what I planned to do on my birthday. I told her that I was giving healing and afterwards I intended staying at the Temple for the service. In fact I wanted to dedicate my birthday to Baba and spend the evening in the spiritual environment. She wanted me to go with her for a meal in a nearby restaurant. I said that I would think about it and let her know. When she telephoned me again on Friday to find out what I had decided, I did not have the heart to disappoint her, so I agreed to meet her at my house after the service when we would go out together.

On Sunday, after healing and the Aarti service, I left the Temple and went with my friend for a meal. On Monday morning 15th July at 9 a.m. Dulcie phoned me saying, "Ruth, why did you leave the Temple yesterday. You don't know what happened after you left". She then related to me what had occurred as follows:

She said that, while sitting in the lounge with a few other people, and some members of Mr. Patel's family, they suddenly heard strong thumping noises coming from upstairs. They knew that no one was there as Mr. and Mrs. Patel were away, so they continued talking and ignored the noise. Still the thumping happened again and then they heard a few strong knocks on the front door. They opened the door, but no one was there. Suddenly Bhavish, Mr Patel's nephew, noticed a wet stain by Dulcie's feet. She bent down, and on examining it she realised it was 'Amrit'. Amrit is a nectar which tastes like honey, has a scent of flowers like jasmine and roses combined. Its taste is indescribable, so absolutely delicious, and is a rare blessing. I have seen it appear on special occasions on pictures of Deities. I have also seen it trickling from the toe of an idol of Shirdi Sai Baba. Mrs Patel had to put a small bowl under the statue to collect this precious nectar and we all had a taste of this amazing 'Amrit'.

Someone then noticed jasmine petals and vibhuti stretching out in a line up to Baba's chair, which stands in the adjoining room where the Temple is situated. One of the ladies present said to Dulcie that she saw Baba emerging from the big picture in the Temple. They were all stunned, and felt greatly blessed and uplifted by this experience.

I felt such remorse that I had not remained at the Temple as I had planned. I could not help the tears that just flowed. I went into my prayer room at home asking Baba's forgiveness. After a short time of praying, I had a sudden urge to go to the Temple, so I picked up one of the beautiful roses that had been given to me for my birthday and drove to Mr. Patel's home.

I arrived at 12.30pm in front of Mr. Patel's house. I knew it was too early to go in at that time. The Temple opened to the public at 3.30 p.m. It was too long for me to wait, so I decided nevertheless, to knock on the door. When Mr. Patel answered the door he seemed concerned at seeing me in such a distressed state and asked what was wrong. While showing me in, I related to him and his daughter Mini how upset I was to have gone out on my birthday and missed the manifestations, which Dulcie had described. Mr. Patel said that he also had not heard from his relatives what had happened as neither he nor his wife was at home. His daughter brought me a vase for my rose, and left me alone in the Temple, closing the sliding glass door behind her.

I placed the rose at Baba's feet, praying and asking Him for forgiveness. I also asked that He give me a sign to show He had forgiven me, repeating this several times while saying that I would not know peace until I had this sign. As soon as I had finished praying, Mr. Patel's daughter, Mini, who was in the lounge adjoining the temple, opened the glass door and said "Ruth, don't move, the back of your T-shirt is full of vibhuti!" As I could not look over my shoulder she took me upstairs to look in the mirror. I was puzzled when I saw it for myself and said that maybe I had dropped some vibhuti on myself when I took some in my hand and dabbed some on my head. She said that this could not be because it had formed in blobs from my neckline down to my waist!

I returned to the Temple and thanked Baba for this sign, though still with a little doubt in my mind. While I was kneeling, Mini opened the doors again and said "Ruth, don't move". I looked at her, very puzzled, asking "what now?" She told me that there was now vibhuti over the white flower hair clip I was wearing as well as down the right side of my hair. This second sign finally convinced me. How well Baba read my mind when I was doubting after the first sign! Once again Mini took me upstairs, I looked in the mirror and removed the flower ornament from my hair to see the vibhuti dotted over the flower and on my hair. I felt happy beyond words and grateful that Baba had so speedily answered my prayer. I now felt at peace.

What can I say about all these manifestations? Everything happened as described. I was under no illusion, no delusion. Everything was real. Others present witnessed and confirmed each event. Most of us, if we see a miracle before our very eyes, will try to find some logical explanation. We refuse to believe our own eyes or admit to what we have seen or experienced, because it is something beyond our comprehension. At first we try to find an interpretation for it in logical or material terms, but these occurrences, being above and beyond the material, are in a spiritual dimension, and therefore the logical mind is incapable of measuring them.

Our intellect finds it hard, even impossible, to accept, and we reject it outright as a clever play of magic, or imagination. But spiritual and material laws are totally different, as is made plain from many of the stories in the Bible. I must confess that at the beginning, this was my attitude. But after years of having seen and experienced the amazing things I have described, I have no doubt whatsoever as to the truth and reality of all I have witnessed. Baba says *"Do not give ear to what others say, believe your own experience, your own eyes"*.

God's love is a divine and unconditional love for which all yearn. Mistakenly, we think of our worldly love of parents, husband, children, friends, as the real love to which we are attached and to which we cling. But we discover that this is only a transient love as our dear ones sooner or later are taken from us, leaving us bewildered, unable to comprehend or accept our loss.

The sooner we come to the understanding that unconditional love comes from God alone, who is the Eternal Love manifesting through our earthly family, such knowledge, such belief, will guide and help us to cope with our sadness and our sorrow. With such knowledge we gain greater peace and understanding, better able to live with the ups and downs of this life, which, however painful, are crucial for our spiritual growth.

And so I relate the blessings I received from Sai Baba, the miracles, and the manifestations that I could not have previously believed possible. A new world had opened for me.

I felt I had to go to India and see Sai Baba for myself. In January 1992 I left London with a group of fellow-seekers, en route for India, and for Baba.

Chapter 9

PILGRIMAGE TO A WORLD TEACHER

Higher and nobler than all ordinary ones
are another set of teachers,
the Avatars of Iswara.
They are the teachers of all teachers,
the highest manifestations of God
through men.

Swami Vivekananda

The awaited day finally arrived. Our group met at the airport on 19th January 1992. There were about 60 of us, including four children. We boarded the aeroplane to Goa in South India, after prayers for a safe journey. The aeroplane was very cramped, not enough legroom, and so I could only sit in one position. I wondered how I was going to be able to bear it for nine or ten hours. We stopped at Bahrain for refuelling and had an hour in the Duty Free shop. We boarded again and arrived in Goa at 9.30 a.m. local time on Monday 20th.

Goa appeared to be a pretty seaside resort, the temperature between 70-80 degrees Fahrenheit. What a welcome change from the cold weather we had left behind in London.

After clearing Customs, we took a bus to the train station and boarded the train to Bangalore. We left at 11.00 a.m. and were told the journey would take about seventeen hours! To our dismay, as we boarded, we saw that it was a dilapidated old train with poor sanitation. Carriages were crowded with people standing or sitting on the floor of the compartments and along the corridors. The smell, noise and heat were unbearable.

After waiting for nearly an hour the train finally started to move. I noticed that the landscape we passed was surprisingly changeable, green fields with palm trees, mud huts and tents, people sitting on the ground doing chores or just staring into space. We passed a few lakes, probably polluted, in which local women were washing clothes while little children splashed about. The children looked malnourished, with legs like sticks and protuberant bellies. Their obvious poverty was painful to see. Cows wandered about freely, some even walking along the railway tracks. Much revered in India, they are left to their own devices. However, in spite of their material poverty, there is, one feels, a richness of spiritual tradition and a sense of acceptance and peace in these people.

With such appalling conditions on the train, I felt that sleep would be a welcome escape, especially as we were told that the journey would last almost a day and a night. The seats in the compartment were wooden and narrow. In spite of being tired and worn out, I found it difficult to fall asleep under such conditions. I put my hand luggage under my head as a pillow, and finally, through sheer exhaustion, dropped off for a short much-needed sleep.

When I awoke, Dulcie and I thought of having something to eat, but we had been advised not to eat anything prepared on the train because of the unhygienic conditions. Fortunately I had brought some biscuits, nuts, dried fruits and cartons of juices with me, which we shared.

I looked at my watch. It was now 4 p.m. It had been five hours since we boarded the train and I still could not pluck up courage to face going to the toilets as we heard that they were smelly and dirty. After ten hours I eventually had to succumb.

We tried to make ourselves as comfortable as possible under the circumstances. We could just about stretch a little on the narrow bench. Suddenly the door opened and a family with two young children, one a small baby, entered our crowded compartment. The result was that we had to sit upright during the entire trip, as there was no space to move an arm or a leg. The baby cried on and off which only added to our agony.

Talking to some people we learned that they had come from the far corners of India, some spending their life-savings just to be at the ashram and receive Baba's blessings, hoping to experience the joy, peace and bliss, which would make their sacrifice worthwhile. Everything is endured with patience and love. They regard Baba as the embodiment of Divinity and this compensates for all the inconvenience and hardship they had to endure in order to reach His presence.

We had been told that the train would arrive at Bangalore by 4.30 a.m. However, as the train was running late, we had to endure the discomfort and hunger for a further three hours, which seemed like a lifetime! We were looking forward to seeing Baba at Brindavan, the ashram near Bangalore, but there were rumours that He might not be there. We would have to wait and see. We prayed that all our difficulties would not be in vain.

We finally arrived at Bangalore at 9.00 a.m. The journey had taken twenty-four hours instead of seventeen! Our luggage was loaded onto taxis for the trip to the Ashraya Hotel. What a joy finally to have a clean bathroom to freshen up in. We felt so dirty from the long journey. It made me realise how spoiled we Westerners are and how we take our everyday conveniences for granted.

Not long after we had relaxed and refreshed ourselves, we had a joyful surprise when told that Baba was in fact in his ashram at Brindavan, forty minutes drive from our hotel.

We were looking forward to our first sight of Baba. Before leaving the hotel our leader divided us into smaller groups, each group wearing a different colour ribbon on their U.K. scarves. We boarded the coach at 7 a.m. in order to arrive and get in line for Darshan at 9 a.m. The ride itself was quite an experience, I found it difficult to get used to the idea that cows walked freely along the roads, pleasing themselves. The roads were full of potholes, so it was quite a bumpy journey as well as a nerve-wracking one, for there seemed to be no specific lanes for traffic. It was a free-for-all. Whoever was the most adept got ahead, with endless horn sounding, and weaving this way and that, narrowly avoiding running over people and animals. On the way, before we reached Whitefield, (the village where the ashram was), I was shocked and distressed to see so many beggars, especially those who had been maimed and who would spend a lifetime begging.

As we approached the gates to the ashram, I saw beautiful children selling flowers, colourful stalls of fruits and vegetables, stalls with trinkets and photos of Baba. Opposite the ashram gates stood a snake charmer playing his flute to 'charm' the cobra, which slowly raised its head from its basket. Once inside the gates, I saw the magnificent Banyan tree under which devotees sit to receive Swami's Darshan.

A corrugated roof extends from under its widely spread branches to give shade to the devotees. The area beneath the tree had been concreted but the rest of the Darshan area was sand. Under the roof in the middle stood Swami's chair and a statue of Krishna (a previous avatar), which is always garlanded with flowers. Also in the compound, in front of the boy's college, was a beautiful statue of Saraswati, the Goddess of learning and knowledge. Further towards the back of the ashram was another archway where Baba lives and has his interview room. Sitting there, waiting for Baba, I admired the whole scene, so different from anything I had previously imagined or experienced.

We had settled down under the Banyan tree on little cushions, cross-legged, when suddenly we saw the orange-coloured robe and Baba's halo of black hair coming out of the gate of his residence, walking towards us but stopping about two hundred yards from where we were sitting. He paused for a few moments, looked at us, and then raised his hand, giving us His blessing. Baba then turned around and went back into his quarters.

From the moment He appeared everyone's gaze was transfixed on Him. I had my camera ready, but did not want to lose a moment of watching Him, so I did not take a photograph. I thought that if He advanced toward me I would have time to take a picture, but it was not to be. However, we were thrilled even for that short glimpse of Him and to have His blessing from a distance. The short Darshan over, we got onto the bus, which was waiting to take us back to the Hotel Ashraya.

We were looking forward to the following day, Wednesday 22nd January, when we would be going to the ashram again, hoping to see Baba and perhaps this time He would come closer to us. We arrived at the ashram and lined up, each group with a different colour ribbon attached to their scarves. We wore these scarves over our kaftans or Punjabi suits so that we would be able to recognise each other among the thousands of people.

Dulcie and I sat in the front line facing the entrance to Baba's house from where He would emerge in about two hours' time, at about 9.00 a.m. Everyone was sitting quietly, either meditating, reading, or talking in whispers. Precisely at 9 a.m. there appeared the small figure of Baba in His orange-red robe, short of stature but somehow filling the area with His presence. He walked toward the other side away from us. However, I was happy that this time I managed to take some photographs of Him.

As He was walking, which seemed more like gliding, or floating just above the ground, He was making the most graceful movements with His hands, sending His blessing to all of us. He first walked to a waiting car, which was allowed admission into the grounds because there was a sick person in it, obviously unable to come out. Baba materialised the sacred vibhuti for him while having a few words with him and his family.

I watched intently as I witnessed the manifestation of vibhuti for the first time. There was peace, love, and so much grace, majesty and dignity emanating from Baba. It is hard to find words to describe Him. After Baba left, most people got up and dispersed, but many remained seated, taking in the energy, meditating, or praying for a while longer.

We returned to the hotel, had lunch, a shower, and a rest, and prepared for the afternoon Darshan. We arrived at the ashram at 3.15 p.m, lined up and waited for Baba to emerge. At 5.00 p.m. He appeared, and, as before, we were transfixed. No one wanted to miss a second of His presence. I held, like so many others, letters given to me, ready to pass to Him, but had no luck this time either. We returned to the hotel.

On the next day, Thursday, Baba's special day, there was a special Darshan with Bhajans (devotional songs) sung to lovely tunes played on instruments by Baba's students. Boys led all the songs from colleges established by Baba. We arrived at 8 a.m. and joined the singing, sitting under the Banyan tree, with its widespread protective branches, until 9.30 a.m., when Baba arrived. He sat on His chair, which was colourfully adorned with garlands, listening to the beautiful Bhajans, moving His hand to the rhythm of the music.

He rose, walked amongst a few rows of devotees, took some letters here and there and was also handed trays of sweets, which He blessed and tossed, back to the crowd. It was a striking spectacle to see Him showering devotees with these sweets, doing it with grace and a sense of fun. Everyone scrambled to catch one of the sweets, which He had blessed. The lucky ones were overjoyed at their 'catch'. He then returned to His chair, tapping His hand to the rhythm of the melodious tunes. Towards the end of the Darshan He went to yet another part of the ground to other devotees, took some more letters, had a word here and a smile there, and then walked or rather glided back to His residence.

Meanwhile we had heard that Baba was going to Bombay for five days for the opening ceremony of the 25th Anniversary celebration of His ashram there. Since Desmond's mother lived in Bombay, Dulcie, Desmond and myself were invited to stay with her in her flat. The rest of the group remained in Bangalore awaiting Baba's return.

Arriving at Bombay Airport in the early hours of the evening, the hot, humid air hit me, reminding me of the burst of sudden heat on opening an oven. Desmond's family were waiting for us with two bunches of red roses, such a nice welcome. They were warm and loving people and made me feel at home.

Next morning, Friday, we travelled by auto rickshaw (a motorcycle Lambretta with a covered back seat) to the ashram, arriving at the gate at 10.00 a.m. Thankfully the ashram was only half full, but by 11.00 a.m. it was filled to capacity. We sat in the third row. Everyone was pushed together in order to accommodate the many thousands who were pouring into the grounds. Waiting for three hours in this confined space and in this heat was truly a test of endurance! We were told Baba would arrive at 1 p.m. Again hours of waiting, but everyone sat in silence in spite of the long wait and discomfort.

As His aeroplane was delayed, Baba did not arrive until 1.45 p.m. I was so hot, I had to fan myself constantly to keep cool as well as shade my face from the scorching sun. Suddenly there was a hush, which always precedes Baba's arrival. When I looked up I saw His car drive past and caught a glimpse of His red-orange robe and crown of hair. He stopped further on and ascended onto the platform of the ashram's hall.

We were all disappointed that He only stayed for a few minutes for the Arathi ceremony (light ceremony), and then left. We had to find our sandals from a huge pile. People were pushing and almost falling over each other to get their footwear.

We finally managed to find ours.

We were exhausted after our morning ordeal. Especially as I had not slept the night before as the sound of the fan over my head had kept me awake. We had lunch and I went to have a nap. Later in the afternoon I decided to buy another Punjabi suit (dress worn over matching trousers). The ashram's rules are strict. Ladies must wear a long skirt or sari and cover their shoulders and busts with a scarf or shawl. We took a taxi to the shopping centre and I bought a pretty Punjabi suit to wear for the celebration.

On the following day, Saturday 25th January, we went to Darshan at 8 a.m. While waiting for Baba, I had a few words with two American ladies who sat near me.

They told me how fortunate and blessed they were to have travelled on the same aeroplane as Baba to Bombay. One of them was lucky to have sat just behind Him, His bushy hair falling over the back of the seat. She said she was gently caressing His hair. Baba did not seem to mind, giving her a sweet smile. When they arrived in Bombay, Baba got up and gave everyone on the aeroplane His blessing. The young lady said she immediately took the loose cloth on the back of the chair on which Baba's head had rested and kept it as a precious memento of an unforgettable journey. Indeed they could not believe their good fortune and thanked Baba for His Grace. It is always interesting to talk to people from all parts of the world, from all walks of life, about their experiences and to see the devotion they have for Baba. I wish I had been able to record all the fascinating stories I had heard.

Monday 27th January 1992 was the ultimate test of endurance. The flat was too small to accommodate all of us so I decided that I would sleep on the covered balcony, which had a fan. The nights were extremely hot and it would be impossible to sleep otherwise. However, the fan, being on all night caused me to catch a terrible cold. It soon developed into an infection of the sinuses and gave me excruciating headaches. As if that were not enough, mosquitoes had a field day on my exposed face. When I awoke each morning I looked as if I had contracted measles. It was a dreadful sight, which depressed me, so I avoided looking in the mirror.

With two more days left in Bombay. Dulcie and Desmond decided to make a pilgrimage to the Mausoleum of Shirdi Sai Baba (a previous incarnation of Sathya Sai Baba), a saint who lived in the village of Shirdi (Picture 6). During Shirdi's life people came from far and wide to seek His counselling and blessings. It had been recorded in writing by His devotees that Shirdi Baba had predicted that eight years after His passing (which happened in 1918) He would incarnate again in the southern part of India to continue His mission of bringing love and brotherhood to the world.

Sathya Sai Baba was born on 23rd November 1926 in a village called Puttaparthi in the south of India, exactly eight years after Shirdi Baba had left His body. Shirdi Sai Baba taught the same principles and virtues as Sathya Sai Baba, Truth, Good Conduct, Love, Peace, Non-violence, and respect for all religions, confirming that, there is only one God, all are

His children, and all are equal. Shirdi Baba was the first to give the sacred ash. Many miracles were attributed to Him, and indeed, as He had predicted, His second incarnation as Sathya Sai Baba continues today, the Divine Mission. Sathya Sai Baba tells His devotees that to complete the work of bringing about the Golden Age of Peace and Love, after His passing at the age of 96, He would reincarnate again as Prema Sai Baba (Sathya – Truth, Prema – Love).

On our way to board the coach which would take us to Shirdi, I felt so ill and in such pain, that I did not think I could face the long trip. However, I did not want to spoil Dulcie and Desmond's plan, so I did not tell them how I felt, as I knew that they would have cancelled the trip.

We boarded the coach at about 5.30 p.m. Little did I then know what I was embarking on. It turned out to be a ten hour trip through scorched fields, mud huts, a panorama of poverty and deprivation, a most distressing sight. Darkness descended and, mercifully, I could see no more. I hoped to be able to sleep through the night and arrive fresh in the morning at Shirdi, but alas that was not to be, as a television in the coach made sleep impossible. We were going on a spiritual pilgrimage of peace, but the television portrayed nothing but violence. The noise of the old engine bumping on the roads was bad enough, but the volume of the television with its brain-piercing sound was altogether a nerve-wracking experience. There was not a single minute of respite from this mind-shattering noise the whole night and not a minute of sleep could be had. I felt I could take no more and wanted to scream with agony, exhaustion and frustration. I doubt though whether my screams would have been heard above the sound of the television. It was ten hours of sheer torture.

We stopped only once on the ten-hour journey at a little isolated café. At that time the television mercifully was switched off. It was silent moments of sheer bliss. But when the passengers returned so did the television. The agony continued as the film on the screen started screeching and blasting my head. Had I known the way to Shirdi I would have jumped out of the coach and walked there! I tried putting cotton wool into my ears but it made no difference. The agony of the trip seemed never to end.

Finally, and thankfully, we arrived at Shirdi Baba's Temple, still dark at 4 a.m. I looked around. A few people were sleeping on the ground under the canopy of stars, lying on thin blankets, their heads resting on their few belongings. It was a strange sight. The poverty was so evident, yet their faith in Shirdi Baba made up for all they lacked materially.

We entered the Mandir (Temple), where the Mausoleum was, and sat on the floor waiting for the service to begin. Many Indian pilgrims sat and waited there with us in their dusty and crumpled clothes and tired appearance. They must have travelled many miles, for many days. I was the only European there. The service lasted an hour and a half. We emerged, tried to extricate our sandals from a pile of dusty footwear. My feet were dirty and I longed to wash them in the little hotel nearby.

As we walked to the hotel, a crowd of beggars followed us asking for food or money. I found myself totally surrounded by beggars touching and pushing me. After the anguish of the bus ride this was the last straw. I broke down in tears and ran away towards the little hotel. I signalled to my friends that I would wait for them there. Dulcie and Desmond went to buy some religious souvenirs and gave some food to the beggars. They later joined me and we sat on the hotel patio beneath a parasol. We had some cool bottled drinks. It was still only 10.30 a.m. and the coach was not due until noon.

What an ordeal these ten hours of travel were. The Temple service lasted one and a half hours, and now a further wait. Indeed this was a true pilgrimage, a test of endurance! Shirdi Baba, during his lifetime, had promised that even after his death, those who came to visit his tomb would have His blessing and protection, and their prayers would be answered.

The return journey was another nightmare. The television was once again blaring away with the same war film. Six more hours of this torture. I could bear it no longer. We decided to get off at the next village and continue the journey to Bombay by taxi. I wondered why I had put myself through this ordeal. It must have been my strong desire to experience the vibrations of this holy place, which I did in spite of all I had been through.

We left Bombay for Bangalore on 28th January 1992. On our arrival at Bangalore airport the same taxi driver who had originally taken us to the airport for our outward flight met us. We had given him details of our return flight to Bangalore and it was so nice to see how reliable he was – a Sai devotee! He told us that Baba was in His ashram at Bangalore. We were delighted to hear this.

Our group leaders, Sandra and Aimé Levy, with the rest of those who had attended the morning Darshan, arrived back at the hotel at 11:30 a.m. The hotel was full and so we had to lodge elsewhere until there was a vacancy.

In the afternoon a taxi took us to the ashram for Darshan, arriving at 3.00 p.m. Everyone sat quietly, waiting patiently for Baba. At 5.30 p.m. He emerged from His residence, giving us a beautiful wave and a smile, both palms fàcing us as He gave His blessings. He then turned around and went slowly back into His residence.

There is something special and magical about Baba. Unless one experiences it, one cannot understand what it is all about. He is the embodiment of pure love, pure grace, pure sweetness, which touches one's heart. His every gesture is perfection in dignity and grace – poetry in motion. I found myself reduced to tears at the sight of Him, and I could see that I was not the only one. It seems to be a common phenomenon for many when seeing Baba and being touched by the outpouring of love, which emanates from Him. One is so overcome and overwhelmed that one cannot help tears from flowing, tears of joy, of expansion of the love in the heart that cannot be contained.

It did not seem to matter that He did not come near us or take our letters, just His beautiful way of greeting and acknowledging us with His lovely smile made it all so worthwhile. The ordeal of the two-and-a-half hour wait in the scorching sun was soon forgotten. When He appeared, our hearts leapt with joy. I felt that my heart too was being captured by Baba. I can now understand all that I had heard and read about the experiences of devotees. Who can awaken in the hearts of so many people from all corners of the world, all religions, all castes, such a universal feeling of pure love and brotherhood? It can only come from one source and that is God, for God is love in all its purity. His wave was like a father and mother lovingly welcoming the childrens' homecoming.

On Friday 28th January we got up at 6 a.m. I had not slept any night since we arrived from Bombay because of a heavy cold and cough and the sinus infection, which was still troubling me. We drove to the ashram an hour later after a hair-raising journey on broken roads with cows, bullock carts and shepherds with their flocks of sheep sharing the road with us. It was incredible how the drivers avoided accidents by a split second. It took our breath away and we tried not to look at the road. Some of us thought it was the last journey we would ever make, but somehow we survived!

At the ashram we were lucky to get into the first row facing Baba's entrance. He came out at 9 a.m. and made His round. He approached one of the ladies from our group, asking where she came from. She told Him that we were the London Group.

He asked how many we were and was told seventeen. He then said questioningly "one-seven?" Then He said "I will see you later". As He walked close by me, about two feet away, I looked into His face and He looked at me at the same time. We had a split second of direct eye contact. His eyes were black and deep like an ocean. I could not see the pupils. I held forward the letters as He looked at me, but He walked on towards His residence. We watched His orange robe until He was out of sight.

I was surprised that at this first Darshan He was so close and even looked at me, but I did not feel any reaction at this stage, even though, on the previous day, when He just waved at us from a distance, many of us had been reduced to tears. Well, perhaps time would tell what it was all about. We stayed in the ashram until after the evening Darshan.

On Sunday 30th January we went to Darshan at 8 a.m. and lined up as usual. We did not get a place near enough to where Baba would walk. There were more devotees there than usual. Bhajans were sung. The beautiful music and devotional songs were uplifting although I did not understand the meaning of the words. It must have been the devotion with which they were sung which stirred the emotions. Baba came and saw a few VIPs who were waiting for Him by the gate. We saw Him materialise vibhuthi by a wave of His hand in such a simple, natural way, that we began to accept it as normal.

Baba walked around, took letters, blessed the sweets presented to Him on a tray and showered them into the crowd. Even that was a sight to behold. The way He does it, with obvious fun, is a joy to watch. He invited two groups for an interview. It was wonderful for these people to have been chosen, as the previous few days Baba had not asked anyone for an interview. When He uttered the magic word 'go', their faces lit up with joy. I could just imagine how I would have felt had it been us.

The following day, at morning Darshan, Baba emerged, walking in His slow and graceful pace, making the rounds and on His way back to His residence passed by where we were sitting. A few hands were outstretched with letters, but He passed them by without taking any. As He approached me I put my hand forward with the letters and He looked at me. For a split second I thought He would continue to walk and not take them since He had not taken any of the others, but to my great surprise He stopped, came forward, and took my letters. I was overcome with joy and bowed my head with respect and gratitude, saying thank you to Him. He then returned to His residence.

The method of selection of the seating in the Mandir ground is to pick a number out of a small bag, which is offered to the first person in the queue sitting outside the Mandir. At afternoon Darshan we drew out of the bag Number 20, which would put us in line twenty. I thought that our line would have no view of Baba, due to the fact that only twelve to fourteen lines were able to get inside the Temple where Baba would be, and the rest of us would sit outside. But when Baba came out of His gate going towards the hall, we managed to get a good view of Him. We even had the pleasure of Him looking in our direction. Later we heard the beautiful bhajan singing coming from the Temple Hall. At about 6.00 p.m. Baba left and again came near to us. I managed to take a few pictures of Him with my camera.

Dulcie had been lucky to be inside the prayer hall and had seen Baba materialise there a silver locket with a picture of Jesus on it for a gentleman from Chile. What a blessing for him to be the only one who was given a medallion materialised by Baba. I hoped that I would be able later to have a look at the medallion.

On Tuesday during Darshan we were about six rows back. Dulcie and others in the group with the red ribbons were in the first row. They had a wonderful Darshan. Baba took all their letters and as He walked by, Baba's toe touched Dulcie's foot and she grabbed the opportunity and put her hands on His feet. She was in heaven. She felt it was a great blessing and I was very happy for her.

The group with the yellow ribbons were from the North of England, Wales and Hampshire. They were invited by Baba for an interview. Afterwards we met one of the young ladies who had been at the interview. She showed us the ring Baba had materialised for her with His picture on it. It was a beautiful ring. She related to us all He had said to her, which was very meaningful regarding her problems.

Another lady from the group had bought an inexpensive ring with Baba's picture on it from one of the stalls in the village. When she was in the interview room she asked Baba to bless the ring. Baba took the ring, held it between His thumb and index finger lifting it up for everyone to see, blew on it three times from a distance, and, 'lo and behold', to everyone's amazement, the ring had changed and was identical to the ring which He had materialised and given to the first lady!

I also learned that the medallion, which Baba had materialised for the gentleman from Chile, was a beautifully crafted ornate silver crucifix. Dulcie told me that this man was deaf and dumb and this gift from Baba brought tears of joy to his eyes. Everyone was delighted for him.

Baba's manifestations have often been compared to magician's tricks, and He has responded thus:

"So far as I am concerned this is evidence of my Divinity. It is not by any means an exhibition of Divinity. All performances of magic, as you know, are done for the sake of income. These are tricks of the magician's trade. They constitute a kind of legalised cheating, the transfer of an object from one place to another by a trick of the hand, which goes, unnoticed. They involve no siddhi (occult power) or miraculous power. What I do is quite a different act of creation. It is neither magic, nor

is it siddhi power either. For one thing, I seek no return. For another, I do not cheat people by transferring objects but I create them. Again, I do so not because of any need or desire of exhibition of my powers. For me this is a kind of calling card to convince people of my love for them and secure their devotion in return. Since love is formless, I do materialisation as evidence of my love. It is merely a symbol".

('God Lives in India' by R.K. Karanjia,
Saindra Publications, 1994)

Baba also says: -

"I give you what you want
So that you may want
What I have come to give you –
Your liberation".

I was still feeling rather low with my non-stop cough and cold, having to blow my nose constantly, which I felt, must have disturbed the people in meditation. I felt depleted of energy. The heat and dust did not help. It was an ordeal to sit through Darshan, but who was I to complain when people had gathered from all over the world, some with young babies, some quite elderly or disabled, to be in Baba's Divine presence. It is incredible the wonderful effect He has on people. He is like a magnet drawing people to His aura of love, peace and bliss, despite all the inconveniences and difficulties, especially for Westerners.

One Darshan stands out strongly in my memory. A few days before our return home, we were sitting on our small cushions waiting with rapt anticipation for Baba's arrival. As soon as we spotted the top of His crown of hair or got a glimpse of His orange robe, the electric current in the air was truly magnetic. All eyes were transfixed on His every movement. One did not want to miss receiving His blessings or experiencing the love which emanates from Him.

Baba came towards us, within a few feet from where we were sitting. I looked at Him, hoping to make eye contact, but Baba passed our row without looking in our direction. As soon as He had passed me, I suddenly felt a tremendous heat inside the middle of my stomach, in the solar-plexus area. The heat was so strong that I instantly put my hand over it, not understanding where it had come from. I had never experienced such a sensation before.

After Baba walked back to His residence, most people got up, but I stayed seated, holding my hand to my stomach as the heat inside me was still intense. When finally I got up, I mentioned to someone what I had experienced. I was told that sometimes Baba sends devotees energy or healing in that way, endowing that particular devotees with what he or she needs. I was also told that I would know what effect this would have on me; perhaps well after arriving back home in England. The heat lasted about half an hour. It diminished gradually over that period. I was also told that the terrible cold and catarrh, which I had suffered during the three weeks in India, could be the cleansing out of toxins in my system.

On Wednesday, Dulcie, Desmond7 and I decided to go to Puttaparthi for the day to see the new Super Speciality Hospital. I especially wanted to see Baba's ashram 'Prasanthi Nilayam', in the village of Puttaparthi where He was born and where He spends most of His time.

The journey took us three hours. The first thing we did on arrival was to visit the Museum, which was architecturally unusual and beautiful, built on the top of the hill. Inside were life-size sculptures and photos of prophets, sages and saints of all the major religions, depicting scenes from the various scriptures and accompanied by quotations from each particular religion. The purpose of the Museum was to foster understanding and tolerance of all the different faiths.

It was incredible how Sai Baba, through His love for mankind, had turned a once unknown, poor village into a holy place of pilgrimage. He has built schools, colleges, a university, two hospitals and clinics all free of charge for whomever is in need. Numerous blocks of apartments have also been built to accommodate pilgrims at a very low cost. In fact, the cost of everything is minimal, including good food in plenty.

Some people live in the ashram permanently, and friends in London had asked us to take a few things for them. These devotees who had lived in comfort abroad seemed happy and content to live simply in one room with the bare necessities. One does not need to have much when you have the peace and happiness from being in close proximity to Baba. The ashram is befittingly called 'Prasanthi Nilayam', meaning 'The Abode of Supreme Peace'. In this atmosphere, material possessions lose their attraction and importance. The Prasanthi-Mandir is the home of Baba in this ashram (Picture 7). This Temple of Supreme Peace, Hall of Prayer, House of Light, Heaven to Devotees, is the abode of Sai Baba.

We bought some books about Him in the Sai Bookshop, and also volumes containing His Discourses. We were surprised at how inexpensive these beautiful books were.

A strange thing happened when we left the bookshop. After buying two books, I walked to the canteen and was looking at the cover of a large book I had just bought entitled 'Sathya Sai The Eternal Charioteer'. I noticed that there were some marks which spoilt the cover of one of the books (on Baba's picture) and the other books were torn on the back cover. I was not happy about this.

After tea we went to meet the resident to whom we were to give a stethoscope donated by the Harrow Sai Centre for the new Super Speciality Hospital (Picture 8). I happened to show him the books and asked if he thought the shop would change them for me. He said that it was not important and that I should leave it, but it was important to me.

After he left I sat down on the doorstep of the bookshop looking at Baba's photograph on the cover, wishing that it was perfect. Suddenly, I heard someone calling me from inside the shop. The man said to me "Let me change the books for you". I looked at him with utter surprise. How on earth could he know that I was not happy with the books and wanted them changed? I went into the shop and the volunteer working there gave me two new books, which were perfect. I thanked him for being so kind and above all I thanked Baba. Who else could it be who surprises His devotees with His knowledge of their thoughts and needs!

We bought some souvenirs and drove to see the new hospital, which is more rightly called a Temple of Healing, a Super Speciality Hospital, where patients receive loving c are, which contribute greatly to their recovery.It is a magnificent piece of architecture. Its design has a spiritual significance based on inspiration from Sai Baba who supervised every stage of the construction. It was built by thousands of volunteers who worked day and night. The miracle of this hospital is that it was built from drawing board to completion in one year, ending on Baba's birthday, 23rd November 1992. The British architect, Professor Keith Critchlow (Director of the Prince of Wales Institute of Architecture in London) said that it would have taken seven years to complete such a project in the West. A miracle indeed. Its design symbolises a sacred tradition believed to engender a divine healing energy, typified by the results achieved, mortality rates and infection being among the lowest in the world. Just recently a second equally magnificent hospital has been completed in Bangalore, serving the people of that region in the same manner.

It should be mentioned here that it was thanks to the initial and most generous contribution of Isaac Tigret, the founder and owner of the well known "Hard Rock Café" who through his love and admiration for Baba's humanitarian work that this hospital was founded. All operations and treatments are free for one and all, rich or poor, from anywhere in the world.

The hospital is more rightly called Temple of Healing for the loving care patients receive there. This no doubt contributes greatly to their recovery. It has the most up-to-date medical equipment. Doctors from America, Italy and other parts of the world come and give their services free. It is Baba's selfless service to the suffering humanity which is so admired and is an inspiration to all who witness this.

A beautiful airport was built near the hospital to make it easier for patients to come from far places. Everything Baba is doing is done with one aim – to serve and alleviate the suffering of humanity. The Prime Minister of India inaugurated the hospital. A second hospital even bigger was completed in 2002 in Bangalore. Many doctors and medical people around the world have come and still are coming to see and admire the success of these hospitals.

As you enter the hospital you step into a most impressive prayer hall above which rises a large dome beautifully decorated with stained glass windows, depicting symbols and scenes from the main religions of the world. From the centre of the dome hangs a breathtaking crystal chandelier donated by Italian devotees.

Although tired, we felt the trip had been spiritually uplifting and rewarding, acknowledging the miracles of Sai Baba. He has transformed an ordinary village into a shining place of pilgrimage to which people come from all parts of the world to experience His divine and unconditional love.

Whatever I write here is but a pale reflection of the actual reality. There is no substitute for personal experience. One cannot but be inspired.

"The Super-Speciality Hospital is a unique example to the whole world. For Baba, every day is a day of Seva (service). He is always there to help the needy, feed and clothe the poor, cure the sick and bring spirituality to everyone".

Sanathana Sarathi

(Monthly magazine of Baba's teachings. July 1997)

On Thursday, as we lined up for Darshan, Baba appeared. Fortunately for the group, those with the red ribbons were called for an interview. The rest of us were disappointed, but one does not question Baba's Will. There were some disabled people in that group who may have needed the interview more than we did. One must trust Baba. He knows our needs.

When the group came out of the interview room, we walked towards them to hear about their experiences. They all seemed very quiet. They had tears in their eyes. We respected their need for reflection and silence.

After a while I asked Dulcie what had happened. She told me that in the interview room there was a young doctor from New Zealand who came in a wheelchair accompanied by his mother. He had been paralysed since an accident ten years before. His last hope was to come to Baba, having heard about His miracles of healing. The mother wheeled him into the corridor where devotees waited before entering the interview room. The group wearing the red ribbons were already waiting, together with the other people, for Baba to come and show them into the room.

As Baba arrived he walked towards the young man in the wheelchair, tapped him gently with His fist three times on each knee saying "Rise up and walk", in a tender but commanding tone.

Miraculously, the young doctor got up from his wheelchair and started walking. He walked unaided into the interview room with Baba behind him. His mother rushed forward wanting to hold his arm, but Baba motioned for her to leave him on his own. Dulcie said that they were all standing there dumbfounded, overcome with emotion at this miraculous sight. There was not a dry eye amongst them.

Baba told the young man that it will take time but he would be all right. Dulcie added that Baba had also materialised a ring and a locket for two of the devotees. When they all came out of the interview room, a few of the group went over to talk to the young doctor who was now walking and pushing his wheelchair!

Someone asked him how he felt about what had just happened to him. His answer was that, being a doctor, he knew that medically, nothing whatsoever could be done for him. The fact that Baba had got him out of the wheelchair and that he was able to walk unaided, was a miracle only God could perform and therefore for him, Baba was God. The whole group who witnessed this miracle came out of the interview, still dazed after their unforgettable experience. It was the immense vibration of Baba's love that healed the stricken doctor.

Friday 7th February 1992 was our last Darshan, as on Saturday we were flying back to Goa. We still hoped we might be called for an interview, but sadly it was not to be. Baba called only Sandra and Aimé Levy, but not the rest of us. Our hearts sank with disappointment and many had tears in their eyes. A few cried openly, unable to control themselves. We had to accept it as, interview or not, one gets the benefit of being in Baba's presence. Just by seeing Him walking close by, one receives the energy and love, which emanates from Him.

Most people feel the changes, which occur in them in a subtle way, but always for the better. I knew I would have to wait and see when I returned home how I would be affected by the experience. One thing is certain with most people, one comes back with greater determination to pursue more seriously the spiritual path. At least, that is how I felt. The first signs one feels is of peace, inner contentment, and an expansion of love, which begins to manifest from within.

On Monday 10th February 1992 we took the flight home via Bahrain, arriving at Gatwick at 7 p.m. and home by 10 p.m. It was the end of a memorable and wonderful trip, the beginning of a crucial stage in my own spiritual progress.

Chapter 10

MY PRAYERS ANSWERED

Bring what you have, namely, your sorrows and grief, worries and anxieties, and take from me joy and peace, courage and confidence.

Sathya Sai Baba

When I arrived home I was still suffering with pain due to the lingering sinus infection. My doctor put me on a course of antibiotics, and within a few days the infection cleared up and I began to feel well again.

On my first visit to Mr. Patel's Temple after returning from India, I told him all that I had experienced, and of the difficult time I had, saying that I don't think I would ever go back again. He just smiled enigmatically. Did he know better?

I began to experience gradual but definite changes in my general attitude. These changes were subtle and slow, but nevertheless significant. I felt more peaceful and contented. Minor mishaps no longer upset me. It seemed that nothing could worry or get to me anymore. My priorities had also changed. I was no longer interested in material things as before or trivial conversations and social pre-occupations, or going to the theatre, watching television, listening to the radio or reading newspapers and magazines. I enjoyed being on my own which I never did before. I wanted to do more meditation and listen to Bhajans (devotional songs), to study Sai Baba's teachings and books about Him.

I felt more secure and self-confident. More importantly, I realised that whatever remained of the pain and stress from my broken marriage had disappeared. A spring of happiness entered my heart, which filled me with Divine love. At times these feelings so overwhelmed me that I was moved to tears, tears of joy out of inner gratitude for my upliftment and newfound happiness. I felt an all-encompassing love towards the whole world, my heart expanding to embrace all humanity, all God's creation. I felt closeness to everyone. All were my family, the world was my home.

There were moments of sheer bliss (ananda), something I had read about but did not understand, and certainly never dreamed I would ever experience. Where had all this come from? Having returned from such an exhausting trip, suffering hardships throughout, why was I now experiencing such bliss? It could only be due to the grace of Baba's Divine Love and His Blessings, which touched me while I was there, without my even realising it.

Some of my closest friends, as well as my son and daughter, remarked on how much I had changed. They told me that the peace and serenity, which showed on my face, gave me a certain radiance. I began to feel Baba's Divine guidance in so many areas of my life. He answered many of my prayers, which were mainly for family and friends. For myself, I asked only for guidance on the spiritual path, for energy to fulfil whatever I had to do in the way of healing wherever help was needed.

Also, there was my great need for someone to help me sort out and organise all the notes I had kept of my experiences over the previous thirty years. I prayed to God ceaselessly for the right person who could assist me. I felt strongly that what I had experienced and was inspired to keep records of was meant to be incorporated in a book. I realised I was meant to write this book. The title 'From Bitter Came Sweet' had filtered into my mind at the crucial moment when I was at my lowest ebb after returning home from hospital following the car accident.

Over the years there was a ceaseless inner urge nagging at me to embark on this task, but I had no idea how to begin or go about writing a book. I felt strongly that recording my experiences might help others to find hope, courage, determination and faith to overcome whatever tragedy or suffering they had to face in life. While in India, I wrote about this need to Baba asking for His help. He took my letter. I prayed to Him at Darshan for guidance in this respect, but nothing happened for some time and I began to wonder whether I would ever fulfil that task. We do not always get what we ask for as quickly as we wish. In fact I had to wait four years! God knows best the right time and the right place when our needs are to be fulfilled, in His time and in His way.

That way came to me one Sunday after we had finished healing at the Temple in Harrow. While sitting in Mr. Patel's lounge, a young lady who came for healing walked in. She turned towards me, and pointed a finger in my direction, saying, "You are going to write a book"! I looked at her in utter surprise, and somewhat shocked, as she continued "and this is not the only book you will write. There will be a second one too, but there are two more events which will happen in your life, and then you will be ready to finish the book and it will be published". She continued, "You must write about this house (Mr. Patel's) and everything that has happened here, also about the healing. Keep a record of the healing successes".

I told her how incredibly right she was, that I was praying to Baba for help as I was in need of someone to assist me in organising my notes and writings so that they could be put together in a book. I asked her when she thought I would finish the book and she answered, "In about two years' time". Her prediction was somewhat optimistic, as the first draft was not completed until 1997, four years later.

I asked her, "Are you a medium". She opened her handbag and gave me her visiting card. She was a researcher at London University. She had a university degree in psychology and was a practising psychic. She had come to see Mr. Patel's Temple, at the same time bringing her boyfriend for healing. In her own words she said, "I saw ash appearing on a photograph as I sat in front of it. I have no doubt that the phenomenon is genuine". These comments were printed in

The Daily Telegraph on 6th March 1992 in an article about Mr. Patel's shrine and Sai Baba.

I continued to heal at the Temple. The Divine vibrations were uplifting to both healers and patients. We were thankful for the many wonderful results, which took place. The stream of patients increased every week. I recall one particular incident indicating the effect the special atmosphere the Temple had on patients. The following is a transcript of a letter describing the writer's experience.

"Spiritual Healing at Wealdstone Sai Baba Centre

01.09.1991

"I had been suffering from chronic gastritis for more than two years and three doctors tried to cure it through their medicine, but in vain, for it got gradually aggravated in spite of the specialist medical treatments.

It was one-month back when I went for spiritual healing, done free of charge as a divine service, at the Harrow Wealdstone Sai Baba Centre on Sundays from 3 to 6 p.m.

I was treated by Mrs. Ruth for about ten minutes, the ecstatic experience of which is deeply treasured in me because I had never experienced such an altruistic love flowing into me from a secular being.

In fact I was subject to a torrent of divine love emanating from a Divine Source through the medium of Mrs. Ruth into my entire spiritual and physical self, transforming myself entirely into the natural state of ecstatic bliss with the graceful receiving of boundless LOVE flowing generously from without. Love from without was received harmoniously by the love within, with the individual soul becoming a part and parcel of the Universal Soul. I felt as if I was enveloped in the bosom of Universal Motherhood. With that motherly love, all my mental and physical pains evaporated and vanished into thin air.

It was an amazing experience to feel the healing power emanating through Mrs. Ruth getting stronger and stronger every second from the very significant moment she started directing deliberately all her benevolent psychic forces into me. By the time she started healing me she had already applied her healing power on a dozen others. The general rule is that the healing power gets depleted to a great extent when it is applied even on one or two. My amazing experience with regard to the healing power emanating through Mrs. Ruth was that the more she applies it, stronger and stronger it becomes, for the healing power I felt flowing through her toward the end was much stronger than it was at the beginning. The strength was so great that I got completely cured then and there.

I tested her cure for one month, taking regularly very hot and sour food, which I could never take under normal medical treatment.

It was to show my gratitude for this miraculous cure that I went to the Sai Baba Centre today. I made an appointment to meet Mrs. Ruth and waited in the queue for more than two hours as the healing centre was so crowded. When I met her at last and thanked her for the miraculous cure, she wanted to apply more healing power on me as a preventative measure.

She started applying the healing power first on my head. I felt a great change coming, not much on my body but more on my mind, where all agonies, depressions, tensions and anxieties were evaporating with the tremendous motherly love that Ruth was applying on me. I let myself go fully relaxed with my eyes closed. Then I started experiencing myself to be within a globe of amber light in the bosom of Sai Baba.

I felt that I was getting spiritually uplifted to a divine level of mentality pervaded by enormous love, compassion, mercy and kindness coming through Ruth.

When she started directing her psychic forces on my heart, I felt my dead parents, grandparents, aunts, uncles, etc. in clean milky white robes emanating enormous love and affection surrounded me. It was a great soothing tranquillity that I was experiencing.

When Ruth stooped down and took my feet into her hands I felt that my feet were in the hands of loving Christ for absolution. What a humility I felt in the presence of holy Jesus Christ.

When Ruth took my hands in hers I felt as if I was in the hands of mother Mary like the lifeless body of Jesus after crucifixion.

Throughout her operation, the ecstasy I felt was inexplicable. It was the ecstasy of altruistic love I was experiencing from within and without.

What I underwent was not the mere healing of my body but the miraculous healing of my spirit being immersed in the UNIVERSAL MOTHERHOOD manifested divinely through Ruth who I think is an embodiment of motherly love, kindness, mercy and compassion. She is not a mother only to me but to all living beings as well. How lucky am I to be embraced by such universal motherhood!

MAY ALL BEINGS BE BLISSFUL

Signed T.S.A.
London NW2

Reading this extraordinary experience made me feel very humble. It reminded me of the dream I had about Jesus and the crucifixion, as well as my photograph in Beirut with the cross above my head. I wondered whether there was any connection.

The prediction of my writing a book started to unfold although I had to wait nearly four long years. One evening while I was visiting my good friends and Sai devotees, Ivan and his dear wife Marguerite (Ivan meanwhile had joined us as a healer at the Temple), I happened to mention that I felt downhearted because I had so many notes and a diary of my experiences over so many years but could find no one who could help me to put it together. It was constantly on my mind. I felt it could be an interesting and helpful book. I prayed to Baba for so long for help, and also had written a letter while in India which He accepted, but so far nothing had happened and no one was in sight to help. Ivan immediately said, "Marguerite used to be a secretary and is now free, I am sure she could help you. She would be very good at that. Why don't you ask her?" When Marguerite came into the room I asked her. She agreed enthusiastically, saying that she was looking for something different and interesting to do, as she was quite bored with office work, which was the reason she had left her job. She said she would love to come and help me. How strange that my prayers and Marguerite's were answered at the same time!!

I could not believe that, at long last, my despair of never fulfilling this task had come to an end. I could finally see the light at the end of the tunnel. I thanked Baba for His help and

Grace. Marguerite turned out to be a godsend. I never dreamt of finding a more helpful, patient and dedicated helper. The added 'bonus' was that she lived just five or six minutes by car from my house.

I must admit that there were moments as we sat trying to sort out all my notes, when I lost heart and voiced my concern, wondering if I would ever be able to complete this difficult assignment. Marguerite immediately reassured me saying that she had no doubt, and her faith and enthusiasm about the importance of the book gave me the will to carry on. Without her help this book would never have seen the light of day.

At times I wondered if I would be able to fill in all the details of important events, which had happened so long ago. Fortunately, while re-living past painful experiences, everything seemed to fall into place like a jigsaw puzzle. This strengthened my belief that I was meant to write this book. Why else would I have kept all those notes, when at the time I had neither idea nor intention of writing a book? It was this inner compulsion and guidance to jot down my experiences and feelings, which I could not resist.

While working together, struggling with an old-fashioned typewriter and my fragments of hand-written notes of over thirty years, which had to be collated, we ended up joking, saying that this task was like trying to climb Mount Everest backwards! I said I hoped we would reach the summit! Was it a coincidence that I should meet Marguerite and that I came to know her and her healer-husband only since coming to Sai Baba's fold? Was it yet another coincidence that Marguerite had just given up her job and was free to help me? Baba says, "Coincidence is God's incidence". When you pray, trust, and are prepared to wait with patience, God's help and guidance are sure to come at the right time.

A few months after returning from my first trip to India, I felt the urge to return again to see Baba. This seemed astonishing to me after all I had been through on my first trip, but the urge to go was strong in my heart and, as Baba says "I am in your heart". I felt it was a call from Him, which I could not resist! Having tasted the nectar of Baba's Divine love following my first visit, I thirsted for more. Soon I began to plan my second trip during December 1992.

I was one of a group of about ninety people on this trip. We were divided into four equal groups. I was filled with the same happy anticipation, as I am sure everyone going to Baba is, whether for the first, or any number of times.

We arrived at Puttaparthi, Baba's main ashram, at the end of a four and a half hour coach trip from Bangalore at about 12.30 p.m. We sat patiently for two hours under the shade of a small tree, our suitcases and luggage surrounding us, while we waited to be allocated accommodation.

The heat of the sun at this time of day is merciless. We were hungry and especially very thirsty. A few people kindly volunteered to get some food and drink from the canteen and brought it to those who were too tired to queue for it. It seemed two very long hours at the end of a tiring trip, but a pilgrimage to a holy place and especially to have Darshan from a Divine Being such as Baba, is not meant to be an easy, light-hearted holiday. One has to be prepared to endure difficulties, hardships and inconveniences as part of one's test of determination, dedication and devotion.

The ashram in Puttaparthi is unique in that it is completely self-contained; providing accommodation, Western and Indian restaurants, shops for clothing, medication, a bank, everything one might need. Volunteers run the shops. Baba has done this to discourage devotees from going out of the ashram grounds, so that they will not lose the spiritual vibrations by going into the hustle and bustle of the village. To benefit from a visit to Prasanthi Nilyam one must be committed to Baba's teachings and put them into practice. This is a spiritual journey, not a holiday.

As one enters through the gates of Prasanthi Nilayam (the Abode of Supreme Peace) all cares and problems of the material world drop out of one's consciousness. With no radio or television and no newspapers to bombard us, it is possible to listen to the 'inner voice' and experience a lightness of heart. One can discover a blissful state and, through this, an expansion of the heart, to love more, and to have greater compassion. This is the beginning of a transformation, which everyone hopes to experience.

At the ashram, outside the Conference Hall, called the Poornachandra Hall, there is a blackboard on which is written every morning a 'Thought for the Day' from Baba for the devotees to copy it into their note books. The following is one I copied on Christmas Eve:

> *'The day on which Jesus was born is a Holy Day. He announced Himself as the Messenger of God. In fact, all humans are born as Messengers of God. The sole purpose of this human career is to propagate the Omnipresence of God, High, Mighty and Glorious. No one has incarnated for merely consuming and catering to one's senses. Human life is much more precious than that. That is why the capacity to appreciate beauty, truth and goodness has been endowed only on man."*
>
> Baba

After a long wait we finally received the keys to our rooms. We were delighted to have been given accommodation in the roundhouses, rather than in the shed. We had just enough time to drop our suitcases and hurry for the afternoon Darshan. As I was leaving my room on my way to Darshan, I wondered whether I should take the letters I was given for Baba. I did not think that on the first day at the first Darshan I would be near enough to the front line to be able to give them to Him. But I followed an 'inner urge' to take them with me all the same, 'just in case'. I quickly returned to my room, took the bunch of letters out of my hand luggage and hurried to catch up with the rest of the group. How happy I was to have followed this 'inner urge' for, quite incredibly, we were fortunate to be seated in the second and third lines, just in front of the Mandir (Temple).

We settled down on the ground, on our small cushions. The area around the Mandir slowly, quietly, filled to capacity. People had come from all countries, all races, and all religious beliefs. These differences were not important, for we all shared one thing in common, our quest and hunger for the spiritual food in Baba's message of Universal love and the brotherhood of all mankind. Baba is the embodiment of pure love and selfless service. One cannot but be touched and transformed by His Holy vibrations and presence.

We sat quietly, meditating or reading, awaiting His arrival. Just a little over an hour had passed when we heard background music, an indication that Baba had emerged from His quarters. At that moment everyone's eyes and bodies turned towards Baba, following His every move with yearning hearts, longing for the love, peace and bliss which He bestows on devotees. He walked slowly and very gracefully, as if floating, towards the seated crowd, approaching in our direction, taking letters on the way

As Baba came closer to where I was seated, He seemed to have stopped taking any more letters, and the two or three ladies on my right did not get their letters taken. A quick thought crossed my mind that when He saw the bunch of letters I had, He probably would not take them either. However, as He approached in front of me, I stretched out my hand and looked at Him beseechingly, mentally pleading for Him to take the letters.

To my utter surprise, He stopped in front of me, took all the letters out of my hand and as I looked straight at Him, He gave me a most beautiful smile. There was so much love in His smile, a smile of recognition, as if to say "I know you, I am happy to see you", a welcoming smile full of tenderness, of a mother greeting her child. My heart leapt with indescribable joy. I was so grateful, happy, and relieved, that Baba had taken all the letters and I would not need to carry them with me to every Darshan and Bhajan as on previous occasions. A feeling of elation filled me, of joy, love, and peace, all rolled into one – I was on cloud nine!

Somehow, it did not seem to matter any more whether or not I would get an interview. I felt that I had already had my private interview and an ' inner view' with the beautiful smile Baba gave me! Baba called some people for an interview. I watched the joy on their faces as they hurried toward the veranda of the Mandir, and I could feel their joy in my own heart, as if I was there with them, sharing their happy anticipation. I felt so blessed. What more could I ask for? But ask I did, although not for myself, which will be evident from what followed.

My first interview came on this second trip. Tuesday 15th December 1992 was the sixth day since we arrived at the ashram. We got into line as usual at 6.30 a.m., again hoping to have a front row when the numbers were drawn out of the bag. During the previous five days we were nearly always at the back where we could hardly see Baba. Our necks had been stretched to their limits trying to catch a glimpse of Him.

The numbers were finally drawn and, 'lo and behold', we got the magic number 'one', which was taken, out of the bag by my friend Dalia. We were ecstatic. We would finally be in the first row and could see and be seen by Baba. We sat silently, each one of us praying and hoping for an interview, although it seemed unlikely because it was near Christmas and thousands of people were in the ashram. We did not have long to wait.

Baba, wearing his orange robe, emerged, walking in His customary graceful way. He came towards us and stopped to ask Sandra Levy, our group leader, how many were in our group. She told Him we were nineteen. He paused for a second and said the magical word "GO!"

We walked to the veranda of the Mandir where He has His interview room and waited there for Baba to finish His round of Darshan. It did not take long, just seven or eight minutes, and Baba returned to the veranda and showed us into the interview room. We entered a small square room. Near to His chair was a curtain leading to a smaller, private interview room. We sat on the floor in front of Baba's chair, the men on His right and the women on His left. As soon as we were all settled Baba entered and took His seat. I found myself sitting at the front by His feet. Dalia sat next to me. We were all elated and in awe to be so close to Baba and have His attention focused on us.

The first thing He did was to come to our side, circled His right hand three times and produced white vibhuti, which he poured into the hands of the ladies present. It was warm and of a coarse texture. We ate this sacred ash made especially for us. He then sat down and, since I was sitting by His feet, I gently took His left foot and held it between the palms of my hands. Dalia followed and put her hand on Baba's ankle. Margaret, a nurse in our group, was gently stroking his leg, and Baba, in His infinite love and understanding, allowed us to continue to touch His feet for at least ten minutes, while he was talking to some of the devotees.

In Indian culture, touching the feet, notably of an elder, is a mark of the highest respect. This practice takes on further significance when one touches the feet of a saint or Avatar, since it is believed to cleanse the effect of one's past sins and it is considered a great blessing. While holding Baba's feet, I was astonished to notice how soft and smooth His skin was since most of His life He walked barefoot. Also, I wondered how it was possible that there was not a single grain of sand on His feet after He had just walked along the sandy grounds from His residence to give Darshan to the devotees.

During the interview He asked an Australian boy, who seemed to be about eighteen years old, a spiritual question to which he did not give the correct answer. He then repeated the question to the rest of us and someone thankfully came up with the right answer. I wish I could remember what the question was, but sitting with Baba and especially while holding His feet, it is very easy for one's mind to be unaware of what is happening around them, so that it is difficult to retain everything that had been said.

Baba then spoke to the Australian boy, asking what he wanted, to which his answer was whatever Baba wished for him. Baba got up and in His usual way circled His right hand three times and materialised for him a beautiful gold watch. This I could see quite clearly as I happened to be sitting just under Baba's hand. Baba called the young man to come forward and placed the watch around his wrist. We all gasped at what we had just witnessed, and needless to say, we shared the overwhelming joy of this young man.

Baba asked another young man what he wanted. He too replied that his wish was whatever Baba would wish to grant him. Baba turned His hand only once this time, and, 'lo and behold', a glistening gold bracelet with Baba's face embossed on it had been manifested! Once again He called the young man from the back row and placed the bracelet on his wrist. The expression on the face of the youth, as he turned to go back to his seat, was one of joy and disbelief that this was happening to him.

With another wave of His hand, Baba produced a Lingam, which He was holding between His thumb and index finger while looking around the room. We wondered who would be the lucky one to receive this auspicious gift. Baba called a lady from the back row to come forward and gave the Lingam to her. Surprise and joy was written all over her face. A Lingam is an egg-shaped semi-precious stone that symbolises the Universe and creation and is worshipped by Hindus in a ceremony with special prayers. When water is in contact with the Lingam, it becomes holy water and is collected and used for healing purposes. As we discovered later, the lady who was given this gift was a social worker involved with terminally ill patients in a hospice in Australia. We found out later that she was the mother of the two young men for whom Baba had manifested the watch and bracelet. What a blessing for that family!

It was awesome to witness how all these things came out of Baba's hand, sometimes with barely a single turn of His palm. Baba asked if we had any spiritual questions. Some questions were put forward, which sadly I did not make a note of. I do remember though that Baba emphasised that there is only one God, of whom we are part. Our body or mind is like the clothes we wear, to be discarded. Our soul is at one with God, and the purpose of our life is to realise this. All things are God and God is love. All we do, think or aspire to must be to realise the God within us. God is our conscience and our teacher, if we but listen. Our body is perishable. We therefore must not attach too much importance to the body, but we must take good care of it, as it is an instrument for His work.

Baba has said, *"There are three of you, the one you think you are, (the physical) the one others think you are, (the mental) and the one you really are – the divine spark within".* He added that the purpose of life is to realise this.

There was much more Baba said. We listened with rapt attention. He put the most profound and complex spiritual concepts in such simple terms that everyone could understand. Baba emphasised that there is only one God and that everything emanates from Him. Each of us is God, but we do not realise it. Baba's mission is to show us the way to perceive this truth, to become the Divine Self we really are.

When people say "my body", or "my mind", who is it, asked Baba, who is claiming ownership of that mind, that body? I understood that what Baba meant to convey was that the body is matter, and the mind only comes into existence through us having a body. But, and this was the crux of His teaching, both body and mind are held together by the power of spirit. When the spirit departs from the body, the body rots and the mind perishes, but the spirit – soul is imperishable.

Baba gave an example to explain the nature of the mind. He showed us a handkerchief, saying that by removing each thread the handkerchief would cease to exist, even though the handkerchief appears now to be a single object. The handkerchief, He said, represents our mind, and the threads represent our desires. When we remove our desires we shall realise our true self, which is beyond the mind, and which is spirit. His equation for life is:

LIFE + DESIRE = MAN
LIFE – DESIRE = GOD.

My understanding of this is that Baba refers to all the base and material desires that afflict mankind. As a spiritual exercise, Baba advises us to meditate on the question "Who am I?" The soul, which is obscured by ego, desires and ignorance, believes that the body is all we are. But the body and all material things perish to dust. The soul lives and takes on another form at the appropriate time and comes back to this world of matter for further lessons and work. Until we realise this, we cannot ascend the spiritual ladder to our liberation, when the ego is no more and all is God. This is Self-Realisation. All the great prophets and sages have taught this, but we are so attached to our form, personality, and material possessions, that we see but a small part of the picture and ignore the real, the eternal.

I listened further to Sai Baba's words. What does he say? He teaches that God dwells in man. He is the conscience. If we would but be silent long enough, we would hear that inner voice guiding us. Yet so often we keep the door of that conscience closed. We do not always like what it tells us to do or to avoid doing. The voice of our ego blocks out the inner voice of Divinity, and so we live in the darkness of ignorance. This cannot last forever, He adds. Every soul will eventually find its way back to its Creator, to a blissful state of enlightenment.

I believe that life is an overwhelming challenge. We either 'catch the tiger by its tail', so to speak, rise up to every challenge, and make the grade by positive thoughts and actions, or else we fail and come back to face all these tests again. This has been proved to me time and again from the trials and tribulations I have experienced.

Baba teaches, "Be in the world but do not let the world be in you". Do everything with non-attachment to the results; dedicate all our work to God the Creator, in a spirit of humility and gratitude. Without God's Grace and Love, we would perish into the pool of more suffering. Humility, I feel, is an often misunderstood word. It is taken by many to mean that one is weak or meek. Baba explains that humility is accepting that you are not the doer, but an instrument, to do God's work. Without admitting to one's mistakes and shortcomings, there can be no progress on the spiritual path. It is therefore necessary to 'crucify the ego', i.e. to cross the I, thus †, before one can become self-realised. All these were teachings we learned at the feet of the Master.

After fifteen minutes of answering questions, Baba asked the UK group into His smaller room behind the curtain where he usually conducts personal interviews and private counselling. After ten minutes with Baba talking to us about personal matters, we returned to the main interview room where the rest of the people were waiting. They too in turn were asked into Baba's private room, all emerging, and faces glowing with happy smiles. To be in Baba's presence, to feel such pure and sweet love emanating from Him, is truly a transforming experience.

At the end of the interview, Baba asked someone from our group to pass Him a red basket, which was on the windowsill from which He took handfuls of vibhuti packets and put them into everyone's hand. The interview being then over, we all got up quietly, each holding in our hearts sacred moments with our beloved Baba. What a day, what a blessing!

At morning Darshan on Christmas Eve, we were again blessed to have drawn row number one. Baba came out smiled, blessing us all. At 10.15 a.m. after morning Darshan we had our last rehearsals for the Christmas Concert at the Poonachandra Hall. In the afternoon we lined up, all dressed in white with flowers provided by the ashram to decorate our hair. It was a sight of purity and of joy. Once again I was fortunate to be in the second row. Baba's chair was placed outside on the veranda in full view of everyone. I was in the Choir and we sang to Baba all the songs we had been practising for a whole week.

Baba obviously enjoyed our singing, moving His hand in tune and swaying His head to the beat of our Christmas songs and carols. While listening to the singing, He was handed a pad by one of the students sitting near Him. Baba looked at it, making some comments, and then patted the boy tenderly on his head. The boy smiled joyfully and returned to his seat. It is always a heartening sight to see how approachable Baba is to his students at all times. The college boys always sit in pin-drop silence around the entrance to the Mandir in their spotlessly white shirts and trousers, their faces expressing deep devotion for the Divine Teacher.

The singing lasted for about an hour. When it ended, Baba stood up and walked along, passing close to our row, saying with concern in His voice how tired we must be after all the rehearsals and preparations. He made a few humorous comments to the people sitting in the first few rows while smiling broadly, and obviously enjoyed seeing us laugh. He returned to the veranda and waved to us again so sweetly, melting our hearts. The atmosphere was charged with the energy of love which made many shed tears of joy.

When the afternoon Darshan finished we suddenly saw the gate at the side of the Mandir open, where a lorry was waiting for the students to unload enormous containers onto Baba's veranda. Within a few minutes we were all given a banana leaf followed by a helping of savoury and sweet rice that was put onto each leaf. What was incredible was how tens of thousands of devotees as well as people from the nearby villages, were all served within about half an hour by the Seva Dal (volunteers).

Baba surveyed the whole operation from the veranda and pointed to areas where people had been overlooked. It was truly a miracle to behold, comparable to Jesus feeding the multitudes, or when God fed the Israelites with manna in the desert. After eating this blessed food, we returned to our respective rooms. I kept my banana leaf as a memento.

On Christmas Day, we rose at 4 a.m. to line up at the Ganesha Gate behind the Mandir at the entrance to the ashram, each of us holding a candle. We walked round the Mandir singing Christmas carols. It was a beautiful spectacle, waves of white-clad devotees each holding a lighted candle, moving slowly in the darkness of early dawn, hundreds of flickering candles, like a moving sea. When we arrived in front of Baba's Temple, we stopped, waiting for Him to appear. We did not have to wait long as the heavy, ornate, silver door of the balcony opened and Baba stepped out, looking at the scene below Him, radiant in the white silk robe He usually wears on His Birthday and at Christmas.

We put all our hearts and souls into the songs. Baba moved along the balcony from one side to the other, acknowledging our singing and sending His blessings to all. After the light ceremony called 'Arathi', we began to move slowly out of the compound humming the carol 'Silent Night'. This was indeed a scene of great beauty and spirituality, difficult to describe but leaving one feeling uplifted and joyful. We extinguished our candles and returned to our rooms. What a contrast to Christmas in the west, full of eating and drinking and dominated by material concerns.

Later that day, at 1.30 pm, we lined up for seats for a performance at 3.00 pm. In the Poornachandra Hall where a

Christmas play was put on by children under the age of fourteen. These were children of devotees who had no previous experience in presenting plays and who had to learn their lines in the very short time of ten days. Parents, or anyone who had a talent in costume making, scenery or props, put their heads together to give the final touch to the scenes.

Each play depicted a well-known story from each of the major religions. First a nativity plays about the birth of Jesus in Bethlehem, then a play about the Zoroastrian religion, followed by the story of Buddha. It was particularly interesting and moving for me to see the play about the Jewish religion, showing Moses coming down from Mount Sinai holding the tablets of the Law. The children, one dressed as a Rabbi, sang a familiar Hebrew song. It was extremely well done and much enjoyed by all of us including Baba, who sat on His rotating chair in the audience smiling and clapping approvingly after every play.

At the end, we were taken by surprise when a large artificial Lotus was carried onto the stage and as the petals fell open, a mini Sai Baba in an orange robe giving Baba's familiar gesture of blessing, stepped out onto the stage. Everybody clapped enthusiastically, including Baba who had a broad and happy smile on His face. This was meant to represent the Age of Baba the Avatar, coming finally to unite and embrace all religions as one through love. Baba walked on to the stage, talked to the children and praised them. Everyone who had a camera took photographs. Needless to say how proud the parents of these children were. We were delighted that everything had turned out so well. The hard work put in by all in such a short space of time was so well rewarded. It was inspiring to see people from every culture, religion and race join together, in peace and in love, to contribute, each in his or her own way, to the success of the project.

While watching the play, I constantly glanced towards Baba. I could see the back of His head. About ten minutes before the end of the play, I suddenly noticed a deep sky-blue halo around His hair over His head, from one shoulder to the other. My eyes were transfixed on this for a few minutes, and then I looked at the stage. When I looked back at Baba, the aura was still there, until the end of the play, when the lighting came back on. The hall was in semi-darkness and only the stage was lit, so the halo I saw could not have been a trick of the light. I have never seen auras before or since.

What impressed me most throughout all the Darshans each day was to see Baba's school children. Most impressive were the hundreds of boys and girls, aged between six and sixteen, sitting two hours or more, waiting patiently for Baba to appear and give them His blessing. They sat in reverence and prayerful silence. It was a moving sight to behold these spotlessly neat and clean children, the girls in white dresses or saris, hair beautifully combed or plaited, the boys in white shirts and trousers. How respectful and disciplined they were. What an example to our Western children!

Chapter 11

MY THIRD TRIP TO PUTTAPARTHI

My affection and love for you is that of a thousand mothers.

Sathya Sai Baba

Mandir Magic

October 1993

Prior to this trip I had been troubled by constant cramp in the calf of my right leg. It was painful while walking, causing me to limp, thus restricting my movements. I was particularly concerned when crossing roads, as I could not hurry or walk fast enough to avoid moving cars. Healing and vibhuti had not cleared the problem.

Before travelling to India to see Baba, I wondered how I would manage to walk fast enough or run, as is sometimes necessary, to take my place at Darshan. Still, I hoped for the best, leaving it to Baba.

We arrived at the ashram in time for afternoon Darshan, hurrying to line up at the back of the Mandir, and hoping to be lucky enough to get inside. This depended on a number one or number two being taken out of a bag. Numbers higher than two would have to sit outside on the veranda, as there is limited space inside the Temple. On this occasion, Baba's grace was with us. Yes, we had the magic number one!

We entered the Mandir and sat close to the college boys who sang the Bhajans. The holy and peaceful vibrations of the Mandir have to be experienced to be appreciated. We sat, shoulder-to-shoulder, knee-to-knee, and were constantly urged to get even closer to one another, to make more room for others. I was filled with an inner joy of anticipation.

As I sat with my eyes closed, trying to meditate and take in the beautiful vibrations while waiting for the Bhajans to start and for Baba to take His place on the throne-like chair, I suddenly felt someone put something into my hand. I opened my eyes and a voice from behind me said "Prasad, Prasad" (blessed food). I looked back and saw this elderly Indian lady smiling kindly at me. I looked around and it seemed I was the only one to get this 'Prasad'.

I hesitated at first to eat it, as no food was allowed in this Holy Temple, wondering also if it was washed and safe, as it looked like a piece of fruit. Still, there was nothing else I could do with it, so I put it into my mouth and realised it was guava. It had a heavenly taste. In fact it was so delicious that I was thinking how I wished for another piece, as I had never tasted any fruit with such an amazing flavour! As this thought crossed my mind, another piece 'landed' into my hand. I turned back, looking at this Indian lady with astonishment. I nodded a "thank you". She again smiled sweetly back at me. I looked at this second piece of guava and felt guilty eating it by myself, so I tore it into two and offered half to the lady sitting on my right, telling her it was 'Prasad'. She too looked at me with surprise, but thanked me and popped it into her mouth. As I ate the second 'helping' of this delicious guava, I suddenly felt someone from the back leaning forward and massaging my right leg, starting from the upper thigh. I turned round in bewilderment, and saw that it was this same Indian lady who had given me the 'Prasad'.

She had, as before, this kindly loving look on her elderly face. I did not know what to do, it seemed so strange, so unbelievable, and to have this done in the Mandir where one sits in silence and reverence. As I looked at her, she just smiled and continued massaging my leg, going down all the way to my ankle. I turned my face towards her, putting my two hands together and thanked her while patting her hand gently, by way of saying, "that will do, thank you".

She smiled, taking no notice of my plea to stop and continued with the massage. The lady on my right seemed a bit annoyed as she had to move herself to the right to let the Indian lady lean forward between us. Twice more I tried gently to get her to stop, but she took no notice and just continued with the massage, looking at me with her sweet smile. I then turned my head over my left shoulder to my young Indian roommate who was sitting to the left of the lady massaging my leg, asking her in a whisper whether this lady understood any English. She told me that it seemed she only spoke Telugu (Baba's native tongue).

After two to three minutes the massage stopped. The lady gestured to me to stretch out my leg. I showed her by gestures that it was impossible since the ladies in front of me were so close to each other that I couldn't possibly put my leg between them. She again pointed to me to stretch my leg again, taking no notice of my explanation. Once more I showed her that it was impossible. Just then, the lady in front of me moved herself a little, making room for my leg to be stretched while turning toward me, and showing me with her hand to put my leg forward between her and the lady on her right!

I stretched my leg, which was a relief, putting it in the space now made for me! How, I wondered, did this lady in front know what was going on behind her and that I needed to stretch my leg? It was one of those inexplicable coincidences, which I had now begun to accept as a higher guidance.

I turned back to thank the Indian lady behind me for her love and care, putting my hands together and whispering a 'thank you'. She promptly held my hands in hers, pointing them towards Baba's chair, saying "for God", meaning of course that I should thank Baba and not her. The whole experience was so moving. I could feel such love surrounding me from within and without, that I was moved to tears. At this moment the Bhajans began and I looked at Baba's life size photograph behind His chair. It seemed His face came alive and there seemed to be so much outpouring of love from His photograph that my heart melted.

Within minutes of the Bhajans starting, Baba entered the Mandir and sat in His chair. I looked at Him and could not stop the flow of tears, tears of joy, of intense love, of deep gratitude. He was moving His hands to the beat of the Bhajans, with such grace, that my heart was filled with indescribable joy.

At the end of the Bhajans, everybody was up on their feet for the Arathi (ceremony of light). I looked behind me, as I wanted to see again the Indian lady and thank her, but was surprised that I could not see her. Perhaps, I thought, she had moved from her place, although it would have been impossible since it was so crowded and the door had not yet been opened. I was so sorry I had not looked back sooner before everyone got up. I would so much have wanted to say a few words to her or just hug her. At the end of the Bhajan however, feeling so full of love, I began to hurry to my room, to record the whole experience in my diary.

Whilst walking, I just I wanted to hug every person around me. I wanted to embrace the whole universe. It was an ecstatic experience. Suddenly I noticed that all the pain and discomfort in my leg had vanished! It was completely healed by the 'magic' in the Mandir. My leg felt as if nothing had ever been wrong with it. It has not given me any problem to this day.

I related this experience to an Indian devotee. She told me that Baba had been known to come in many guises to heal, help, or save a devotee in time of need or danger, disappearing from the scene once help had been given. I pondered on the old Indian lady who had disappeared before we were able to move out of our place. Well, this seemed a possible explanation, shrouded in yet another mystery known only to Baba.

Arriving back in England, I still felt the love and energy I had received in the Mandir. Words fail me to thank Baba for His blessings and Grace. This was my first remarkable experience on this trip.

With Love from Baba - November 1993

My second experience is a moving account of how Baba demonstrates His omni presence. He is everywhere, and knows everything, including our innermost and unuttered yearnings and wishes. However, whether those wishes are fulfilled, is a matter for His Grace, and the time and place are entirely of His choosing. We must have implicit faith and trust that He knows our needs and, hardest of all, to be patient! "With love from Baba" is an extraordinary experience of a prayer answered and the realisation of such Omnipresence and Grace.

As soon as I arrived at the ashram I had in mind to buy a life-size photograph of Baba in His white robe, which He wears on His birthday. I wanted to bring it back with me to London for the celebration of Baba's 68th birthday, which we were having upon my return at the Harrow Leisure Centre.

After a couple of days, having settled down, I went to see Baba's photographer who lives in the ashram. I asked him if he had such a photograph. He told me that he did and went into the next room; bringing exactly the one I had in mind. It was a beautiful photograph of Baba standing smiling in His white robe, with a decoration of coloured garlands above His head.

I told the photographer I hoped Baba would sign it and asked him which pen I should buy for this. He told me to buy a pen called a 'permanent marker' as it dries immediately and would not smudge. The photographer put the picture into a cylinder so that it would not crease. I was now ready. All I needed was an opportunity to be near enough to Baba to ask Him to sign it.

At every Darshan and Bhajan I asked Baba mentally and also wrote Him a letter, which He took, that I would so much wish Him to sign the photograph, 'With Love Baba'. I felt this would be His message of love to all the devotees who would be at the birthday celebration, and later this photograph would be put in the beautiful Temple at Mr. Patel's house in Harrow.

I took the photograph with me to every Darshan and Bhajan. Twelve days elapsed but nothing happened. On Tuesday 2nd November as we lined up for Bhajan in the afternoon, our group leader, Niraj, suggested I should give him the photograph and he would try to get Baba to sign it on the men's side as they seemed to be near the front line on many occasions. I gave him the photo and the pen and wished him 'good luck'.

At the end of the Bhajan, Niraj came to me with a big smile on his face and said that Baba had blessed the photograph, by putting His hand on it twice, once as He walked past and once when He walked back again. Niraj said that Baba was smiling while touching the photograph. Niraj added that now that it had been blessed, I should leave it in my room. I was of course delighted and very grateful that Baba had touched and blessed the photograph, but still I could not help wishing that Baba would sign it as I felt it would make everyone so happy to actually see it in words.

I continued to take the photo with me as before, still praying, still hoping. I even went to see Baba's personal assistant at the ashram, Mr Narayan, to ask for special permission to sit in the front row, explaining that, since we were going home in a few days, I would be grateful if I could be given the opportunity to sit in the front line so that Baba would be able to sign the photograph. I was given permission and was seated in the first line opposite the verandah of the Mandir. The rest of the group sat at the back.

When Baba emerged, He walked towards where I was sitting. I was all ready with His photograph on my lap and the pen in my hand. As He approached, I thought, "here at last was my opportunity", but suddenly He looked in the opposite direction, turned round and started to walk to the other side and my last chance had slipped away! This was a definite and final indication for me that Baba was not going to sign the photograph. I resigned myself to it and left the photo in my room. Nevertheless, I was grateful at least that I was not going back home completely empty-handed, since Baba had blessed the photograph.

Over the last few days it was inspiring to hear Baba's discourses transmitted by microphone from the Mandir, and His leading the Bhajans in His sweet melodious voice. Even a downpour of rain did not deter us even though we were soaked to the bones. Many left, but for me His singing filled me with the Divine vibrations of His voice, that brought tears to my eyes. I could have remained there all night, however soaked I was.

We returned to England a few days before Baba's birthday. The next day, I went to Mr. Patel's house to give him the photograph, telling him that it had been blessed by Baba, although I was sorry that He hadn't signed it 'With Love', as I had so much wished. Mr. Patel smiled, saying it did not matter. He was happy that Baba had blessed it. The picture was to be framed and taken to Harrow Leisure Centre for the Birthday celebration.

Hundreds of devotees turned up to celebrate Baba's 68th birthday, on Tuesday 23rd November 1993. They came from far and near. I was one of the volunteers who had packed the food into little packets, which were to be distributed at the celebrations. As we unwrapped the sealed paper covering the food, we were awe-struck to see that all the food was covered with vibhuti! This was amazing as the ash was beneath the sealed cover. His photograph, which was displayed at the entrance to the hall as well as the decorative balloons, were also covered with vibhuti. This again made us realise His Omnipresence.

The celebration was a great success. The photograph I had brought, as well as other photographs of Baba, was taken back to Mr. Patel's Temple. The next morning my photograph was again covered with vibhuti on Baba's folded hands. How this occurred remains a mystery and a wonder, to me and others to this day. His Presence seems unlimited by space and time.

On the following Saturday, 27th November, I had to travel abroad to visit my mother in Israel. I was away for twelve days, returning to England on Thursday 9th December. The following Saturday, 11th December, I went to the Temple at Mr. Patel's house for the service. When I entered the Temple, the Gayatri Mantra was being chanted so I quickly sat down, closing my eyes. The thought came to me as to where my photograph had been placed and whether any more blessings of vibhuti had appeared on it while I was away.

I wanted to open my eyes and look around for it, but a thought flashed through my mind saying, "Don't open your eyes yet – wait". I answered that thought, saying, "Okay, I will wait until the end of the service". But halfway through, I could not resist the temptation to peep, and opened my eyes. I saw the photograph hanging near Baba's chair by the window. I could see the vibhuti on His folded hands, which had been there before I left, but also noticed vibhuti near the end of the robe, just above the ankles. I thought that this must have happened during my absence.

When the service ended someone went toward the photograph saying that the vibhuti on Baba's robe by the ankles had just appeared during that very service and that it had not been there before the service had started. Mr. Patel confirmed this. He noticed that it was signed 'Baba' in vibhuti. He called me to look. As I approached I saw distinctly Baba's signature. I was stunned, as was Mr. Patel and everyone else.

Mr. Patel turned to me saying, "Ruth", you asked Baba to sign the photograph in Puttaparthi and He came and signed it here. He waited until you came back from your trip to sign it!" Baba could have done it at any time during the twelve days that I was away. The fact that He did it on my return, and on the same day I visited the Temple, moved me beyond words. I felt such gratitude and wonder.

I turned to Mr. Patel who was standing beside me smiling and gave him a hug. A few minutes later, as I recovered my composure, I turned to Mr. Patel and told him how happy I was that Baba had signed my photograph (Picture 9), but I said with slight disappointment, "Baba did not sign it 'With Love'". Having just uttered this, I immediately regretted saying it and promptly apologised to Baba for my ingratitude. I felt guilty and sorry, for in my heart I was truly touched by Baba's grace.

On Tuesday 14th December, I received a call from Mr. Patel asking me if I was coming that evening to the Temple. I was surprised by his call, as he never telephones anyone to ask if they are coming or not. The Temple is open to everyone from 6.25 pm to 7.30 pm. When I asked him whether anything special had happened, he said, "Just come". I said I would.

When I arrived there were a few people in the dining room. Looking at them I could see smiles on their faces. Immediately I felt that something must have happened. When I asked why they were smiling, they told me to go inside the Temple and look. I wondered what it could be. Surely not my photograph, since Baba had already signed His name on it with vibhuti two days before. Perhaps there was some other manifestation, as so often happens there.

I took the hand of one of the ladies standing next to me, and asked her to come with me. As we walked into the Temple, I looked around and faced the photograph I had brought from Puttaparthi. I could not believe my eyes! The 'Baba' in vibhuti that Swami had signed two days earlier, had disappeared and instead I saw the words 'With Love Baba' written in big orange-coloured letters across the photograph.

I was dumbfounded. It was unbelievable, incredible. But there it was in full evidence, Baba's Grace at the place and time of His choosing! How can I ever doubt after that? He knew all along what I had wanted and what I had prayed for.

Answering my prayer in this way was meant to dispel any doubt in anyone's mind of His Omnipresence. I know it to be so, as Baba Himself told Mr. Patel in an incredible encounter.

My eyes remained transfixed on Baba's signature. There it was in big orange letters. I cannot express how I felt. It was beyond words. How elated I was, that He so lovingly obliged and altered the previous signature of 'Baba' in vibhuti to replace it with 'With Love Baba' as I had so much wished (Picture 10).

Turning to Mr. Patel I asked him to tell me how and when it happened. He told me in a few words, but I wanted to know in detail, so I arranged to visit him at a more convenient time when we could sit and talk without interruption.

I remember that before I left on my trip to visit my mother, a message with the figure of '69' in vibhuti appeared on a glass surface which was lying at the Temple in front of Baba's photograph. It was written in such a way that it also looked like the figure '8' (perhaps indicating Mr. Patel's house being number eight). At the side of this figure was a message in the following letters in vibhuti: B C O N, which Mr Patel said meant Birthday Celebration Organise Now. It was with regard to Baba's next two birthdays, 69th and 70th birthdays, which would need a lot of preparation as Baba had told him there would be a much bigger attendance of devotees. Also there were symbols of different religions in vibhuti on the glass plate. Since Baba always says, "Unity is Divinity", this must have been His way of emphasising it with these symbols.

A few days later Mr. Patel related the following to me. While he was sitting in meditation on his own at the Temple on Monday afternoon (13th December, 1993), Swami suddenly appeared to him in His full form, speaking about the future celebrations of the 69th and 70th birthdays. As Baba was giving His instructions, talking to Mr. Patel at length about various matters relating to the Temple and the organisation, a thought came to Mr. Patel whether the people and others of the Sai family would believe whether this message and these instructions were in fact coming directly from Baba Himself. Suddenly, the thought still in his mind, Baba interrupted his thoughts, saying, "Doubts, doubts, doubts". Baba then went toward the picture hanging by His chair, which I had brought from Puttaparthi, saying, "This picture needs to be signed, and which I am signing now!" Mr. Patel was surprised, as Baba had already signed the photo two days previously.

Baba then raised His hand across the picture at a little distance from it, and the vibhuti with the signature 'Baba' (from two days earlier) which was on it, instantly disappeared as if sucked back into His hand. Swami then raised His hand again and it appeared as if He had a pen in His hand, but it was really with His index finger, that Mr. Patel said he saw Baba sign in large letters across the photograph 'With Love Baba', in sandalwood paint.

Mr Patel was stunned and in awe at Baba's appearance, because although He appears to him on many occasions, Mr. Patel said that he had never seen Baba sign a photograph in his own home. Baba then turned to Mr. Patel saying "NO MORE DOUBTS". And added "Swami is everywhere!" after which He 'left'. The whole house was suffused with the smell of sandalwood.

Mr. Patel waited until the signature was dry, then looked for a piece of Perspex to cover it. Strangely enough he found a piece of Perspex the exact length and width of the signature! This was promptly put over it for protection. Mr. Patel made a note by the signature of the day and exact time of this happening. It was Monday the 13th December 1993 at 2.43 pm.

This is the story Mr. Patel related to me. We were both full of awe and devotion at this extraordinary manifestation by Baba in Mr. Patel's Temple. So often we cannot understand the spiritual exaltation of those Shining Beings that come to live amongst us and act as guides and an inspiration as to how we should conduct our lives.

> *"The Lord has to come in human form and move among men, so that He can be listened to, contacted, loved, revered and obeyed. He has to speak the language of men and behave like a human being, as a member of a species. Otherwise, He will be either negated and neglected or feared and avoided."*
>
> *Sri Sathya Sai Baba*

Chapter 12

UNEXPECTED GRACE

Come to me with empty hands and I will fill them with my Grace.

Sathya Sai Baba

After my third trip, I thought this would be my last one, but it seems that the magnetic spiritual cord attached to Baba was beginning to pull me back again to the 'Abode of Supreme Peace'. Once one goes through the gates of the ashram, all worldly and material attachments, concerns and worries melt away. One is transported to another dimension where the higher values of life such as love, compassion, truth, service and universal brotherhood, are experienced. It cleanses and purifies the soul.

We come to be overhauled from all the knocks, hurts and sufferings we have been through in one way or another. Truly I return from each pilgrimage recharged and rejuvenated. This I also hear from devotees who come year after year from all parts of the world, making all kinds of personal sacrifices to be there, to be recharged physically and spiritually. One must have a deep yearning for it and be prepared to make many sacrifices. Baba says, "*Come, test, inquire, taste, experience...*" He also says that no one comes to Him unless He calls them.

So there I was again, October 1994, for the fourth time at Heathrow Airport, meeting with the rest of the group on our way to Baba. A voice came over the loudspeaker, announcing that our flight would be delayed by at least an hour – this turned out to be four hours, two hours in the departure lounge and two more hours inside the plane, which showed no signs of moving.

We asked the aircrew the reason for the delay. They could offer no explanation. They could find no mechanical fault. They were baffled why the plane just would not start. We were anxious to be airborne but were concerned about the undetected problem and our safety. Also we were concerned about our connecting flight to Madras upon arrival at Delhi. From Madras we were to take another plane to Bangalore. Still, events were out of our control and I surrendered the situation to God, praying for a safe flight.

Finally, after two long hours of waiting in the plane, we were told that we were taking off. By the time we arrived at Delhi, we had missed our connection to Madras and stayed overnight at a hotel there. It was decided that due to the delay we would leave out Madras and fly directly to Bangalore.

When we boarded the plane to Bangalore in the morning, we read the local newspaper. We could not believe our eyes as the headlines were all about a dreadful cyclone raging in

Madras, causing havoc and paralysing the city as houses caved in, resulting in electrocution due to falling electric poles. Many people were feared dead. We realised then why we had had an unexplained delay at Heathrow. Had our flight left on time, we would have arrived in Madras in the middle of this terrible cyclone. Baba grounded us so that we would miss the catastrophe in Madras. This was no coincidence, but the intervention of our Divine protector. Of this we had no doubt. The following article is taken from an Indian newspaper documenting the severity of the cyclone:

> ***Cyclone claims 25 lives in TN***
>
> Press Trust of India
>
> Madras, Oct. 31 1994
>
> *TWENTY-FIVE persons were killed in the severe cyclone storm and the torrential rains that lashed Tamil Nadu since yesterday.*
>
> *Sixteen persons were killed in house and wall collapses and due to electrocution in Madras city. The worst case was at Pulianthope here, where eight members of a family were buried alive when their house collapsed.*
>
> *According to official sources here, the storm crossed the Madras coast between 06.30 hrs and 07.30 hrs and lay centred 50 kilometres off Madras at 08.30 hrs. Though the cyclone has weakened, rains are predicted for another 32 hours.*

We stayed two days in Bangalore to rest and do our shopping so as to be ready for our journey to Baba. We travelled in a convoy of taxis, which took about four hours over rough and bumpy roads. I had been given many letters from devotees to give to Baba. Each of them would be anxious on my return to know if He had taken their letters, some from very sick people. I took the letters with me to every Darshan and Bhajan for a whole week, but Baba passed me by on many occasions, took letters from people around me, but mine were not taken.

On Tuesday 8th November Baba again passed me by, taking letters from ladies sitting near me, again ignoring my outstretched hand and my beseeching look. This time I was very upset as I felt He would just not accept these letters and I did not know how I could face all those people on my return and disappoint them. As I thought about them I cried silently. An Indian lady near me patted my hand, saying, "Don't cry, and just continue to pray with love and faith and you will see that Baba will take your letters".

When the morning Darshan ended, and most people went for breakfast, I decided to forego breakfast and move to the front row as soon as people vacated their places. Luckily I was able to do this, waiting from 7.15 am till 9 a.m. for the start of the Bhajans. After the Bhajan, Baba sometimes picks the odd letter on His way back to His residence, and although I was hungry and thirsty I did not want to miss any opportunity to give Baba the letters. The front row was the best place to be where He would pass close enough for me to hand them to Him.

At the end of the Bhajans, Baba came out from the Mandir onto the veranda looking around at the crowd of devotees. I noticed that He looked directly at me. Baba stepped down from the veranda and walked in a straight line in my direction. I sat motionless, holding my hands together in prayer with the letters in my lap, my eyes focused on Him the whole time.

To my surprise and astonishment He came and stood directly in front of me. I raised my eyes to look up at Him, my heart pounding. I was awestruck at this most unexpected Grace. Baba looked straight into my eyes, asking softly "Where do you come from?" I was quite numb with shock by His Presence, so I stuttered, "London". He then asked "How many?"

My mind was paralysed and I could not remember the number of people in our group. As I hesitated a girl in our group whispered to me "Sixteen", so I repeated "Sixteen". He then said something, as He walked away which I did not hear. One of the girls in our group said to me, "Did you hear what Baba said?" I answered, "Yes". He asked where we came from, and how many". She then said to me "Didn't you hear Him say 'interview this afternoon?" I was stunned and asked, "Did He really say that?" A few of our group who were sitting around me said that they all heard Baba say this. It seemed that everyone heard except me, I suppose the shock of Baba talking to me just turned my mind blank.

No need to say how excited and overwhelmed we all were. Immediately a thought came to me. What would happen if in the afternoon when we draw out the numbers we would not be sitting in the front row and Baba would not see me? There were other British groups there and we might miss the opportunity.

An idea came to me to ask our group leader, Sandra, who sits at the entrance to the Mandir with the VIPs, to ask permission from the principal Seva Dal (volunteer) in charge of the Mandir area for special permission to sit in the front row, explaining to her that Baba had spoken to me after morning Darshan promising an interview in the afternoon. I told Sandra to tell her that the group would draw their number as normal and sit accordingly. At least if Baba saw me when He passed He would call us for the interview. I did not want to miss this last chance. Sandra said that she would ask for me and that when we came to line up in the afternoon I should come to see her and she would tell me whether permission was granted.

Before going to afternoon Darshan it began to rain, so we took our raincoats with hoods. I felt downhearted thinking that as we would be covered in our raincoats, Baba would not see our group scarves and we could miss the chance of an interview. I prayed for the rain to stop. Just as we started to line up, the rain stopped!

We sat down in a long line and I got up to ask a nearby Seva Dal whether I could speak to Sandra who was sitting inside the Mandir ground. I explained that Baba had promised an interview for our group. She gave me permission to go. I got up quickly and climbed up the few steps to the open space in front of the Mandir, when, whoops! I slipped on the wet ground and injured my knee, blood seeping through my white Punjabi trousers. In spite of the fall and injury I did not feel any pain. A couple of Seva Dals came running to ask if I was alright, suggesting I should sit down and take a few minutes rest and offering me some vibhuti. I thanked them but said I was fine and wanted to go straight away to Sandra to find out whether permission had been granted for me to sit in the front row.

In the Mandir ground I saw Sandra waiting for me. She said that permission had not been granted, saying that the Seva Dal had indicated that I would just have to sit with my group wherever we were placed. If Baba wanted to call us, he would do so from wherever we might be – all was down to His will. I walked back to join my group with my head hanging on my chest thinking, 'Oh well, at least I tried, and it is really up to Baba now'.

When I came down the steps to join my group, I noticed that the numbers had already been drawn. I did not believe my eyes when I saw number '1' placed in front of the line on our left, so I asked the lady from our group sitting in front what number we had? She told me that both lines, ours and the one to our left, were going together as line number 1, however, we were supposed to follow behind that line. This would place us in the second row inside the Mandir. Still, I was beside myself with joy at this unexpected blessing. It was an incredible blessing, that with thousands of people all hoping and praying to draw the number one line, we actually got it.

As the line on our left got up to go in first, the Seva Dal in charge of order and discipline pulled me up by the hand telling me to get up. I looked at her, astonished as I heard her say to the lady at the very front of the first line, "I want this woman (referring to me) to go in with you because Baba promised her an interview", placing me in front of this lady. I could see from the expression on her face that she was not very pleased, but she could not object.

I was flabbergasted, to say the least, as it is almost unheard of for such a thing to happen. So there I was, the first to enter the Mandir ground and I could pick my seat in the very spot where I was in the morning! My gratitude to Baba knew no bounds. Who else could arrange such a 'play'? The whole drama from start to finish was too incredible to be 'chance'. I settled down on my little cushion, my heart leaping with joy. I had all the letters with me and I thought 'well, now at least Baba will take my letters'.

He came out walking along the first row. As He approached in my direction I noticed that a lady four spaces to my right was also wearing a UK scarf (she was from another UK group). I saw her speak to Baba and I gathered that she was asking for an interview. That minute I felt that we would probably miss our opportunity, as Baba would call her group thinking they were part of our group. How wrong I was.

I saw Baba motion to her with his hand, as if to say 'wait, wait' while He looked in my direction and our eyes met. He proceeded to walk and stopped in front of me. I immediately handed Him all the letters, which He took. He then said the magic word everyone dreams to hear "GO!" I was overcome and fell forward and touched His feet in gratitude.

I remained seated for a few seconds waiting for Baba to walk past me before getting up. Baba took one step past me, and then looked back, seeing me still seated he motioned with His hand to me, saying, "Go, go". I got up there and then, the rest of the group following behind me. We walked up onto the veranda of the Mandir where we awaited Baba's return after Darshan, when He would call us into His interview room.

The ladies sat on one side of the veranda with the men opposite. One of the men in our group was in a wheelchair. I looked at the expressions on the faces of the men. Their eyes seemed full of wonder, looking all around as if to say, 'are we really here and actually going to have an interview with Baba?' To see their excited and happy faces was truly a tonic. I felt even more elated for them as, apart from one man, the others had never had an interview. They could not believe their luck.

We did not have to wait long. Baba came back showing us to His room, men first, the ladies following. Baba waited at the door until we were all inside. He then entered, making sure we were all settled comfortably. I sat next to Baba's footrest, which was a cushion made of red velvet. Baba stood right in front of me and, as I looked up at Him, I saw Him make three small circular movements with His right hand and out poured white vibhuti which He dropped into the palms of each of the ladies in the room.

We all ate this auspicious, warm, snow-white vibhuti. To my surprise and joy Baba put His hand on my head (this is something I so much wished Him to do as I was hoping that the energy from His hand would heal my incurable scalp condition). As Baba took His hand away from my head, I gently took hold of His hand and kissed it. His beautiful and graceful hands always fascinated me.

Baba then sat on His chair, and, being seated just at His feet, I bent forward and kissed His left foot, which was close to me. I then put my hand on His foot, keeping it there while He talked to us about the human ego. He said that one of the most important things we should do is get rid of our ego, as it stands in the way of our spiritual progress. He also said that each and every one is Divine and that we are in fact God, but not aware of it. He had come to lead us back to Godliness. He repeated this, emphasising the words "You are God", in such a way that it made a very strong impact on all of us. Later, discussing the interview, everyone confirmed the deep impression His words had made on them.

Baba looked down at me and noticed the silver ring I was wearing which had His picture on it, asking me "Who is that?" I smiled but did not answer, knowing that He was just humouring me. For a split second a thought flashed through my mind that perhaps He would ask me to hand Him the ring and He would blow on it and change it into some other kind of ring, as I had seen Him do in a previous interview. Alas, this did not happen. He then made a circular movement with His hand, palm down, and, lo and behold, He manifested a silver and gold ring which He threw to a lady behind me, who caught it just in time. He asked her to pass it around for everyone to see. He asked for the ring to be returned to Him and He put it on the finger of a young man in the group. The look on the face of this man was a joy to behold. Baba gave him a sweet smile that must have put the man on 'cloud nine'. The ring had the face of Shirdi Baba (a previous incarnation of Baba) on it.

Baba then manifested another ring, which He gave to the man in the wheelchair, who was equally overjoyed to receive such an unexpected gift. Baba called an elderly lady from the back row to come to Him. He asked her, as He often does to devotees, "What do you want?" She answered, "I want you, Swami". Baba smiled at her and made the usual movement with His right hand, manifesting a gold ring with an 'AUM' sign on it. The AUM sign is an auspicious symbol signifying the sound of creation. He put the ring on her finger and she too looked at Him with tears in her eyes and asked to touch His feet, to which He gave permission.

Baba stood up and extended His right palm facing us as if in blessing, saying "You see this hand, there is nothing in it", then turning the hand so His fingers were now downwards still facing us. He then pointed to His right palm with the index finger of His left hand, saying "But *everything* is in it", signifying that from the palm of His hand all things could be created. He said this so naturally, but there was great power behind these words.

He asked us "What is bhakti?" I answered "devotion". Someone else said it was love. Baba gave more of His spiritual teachings. I felt He was looking straight into my eyes, even though He was addressing the whole group. I had such a warm feeling inside me. I felt Him to be like a father to me. It made me feel so much at home and relaxed, different from my first interview, when He never looked at me or spoke to me whilst I sat at His feet in awe, tongue-tied, my brain not functioning.

Subsequently He took an Indian couple into His small interview room. As He got up, I felt an irresistible urge to put my hands on His red velvet cushion that was his footrest. I felt it would be full of energy since His feet always rested on it. I placed my two hands on the cushion and kept them there until Baba returned into the room. While my hands were on the cushion I was completely oblivious to anything happening around me. I could feel a strong vibration, as if an electric current was going through my hands. This current was constantly vibrating. The pull of the cushion on my hands was exactly like the attraction of a powerful magnet. I could not lift my hands from the cushion. This reminded me of the feeling I once had with the Egyptian healer, Mr. St. George, when he held my hand and filled me with the magnetic current, which saved my eye.

On returning to the room, He looked at me and said, "There is something wrong with your eye", pointing to my right eye. I said, "Yes Baba, I had an accident and I cannot see with this eye". He then very tenderly said, "I will help". He put His hand on my head again and said softly, "I bless". I again took His Divine hand into mine and kissed it. I was overwhelmed when He said the words "I bless". These words touched my heart deeply.

My Israeli friend Dalia, sitting next to me, gave Baba a piece of paper on which she had translated into Hebrew one of Baba's sayings, which was meant to appear on the front page of the first book about Baba which Dalia had translated into Hebrew and which was to be published in Israel. She also showed Him a picture of Sai devotees in Israel watching a video about Him at one of their meetings. Dalia asked "Baba, please bless it for Israel". He took the sheet of paper and pen from Dalia and signed it 'With Love and Blessings, Sri Sathya Sai Baba', then returned the pen and paper to her. Dalia looked at Him, saying "Thank you Baba". He replied softly, "Why thank me, it's my duty".

Suddenly He got up, walked to the other side of the room, switched on the ceiling fan and returned to His chair. We all felt quite hot in the room and Baba, always the caring host, wanted to make us feel more comfortable, saying "Is it better now?" We were surprised He did not ask someone near the switch to turn the fan on instead of doing it Himself, but it is typical of Baba always to set an example. Because of His fatherly way and tenderness, I felt that I could ask Him anything, so when there was a pause in His talk, I said, "Baba, can I ask you something?" He looked at me and waited for what I had to say, so I asked, "Could you please give me energy for my healing work?" He replied immediately, "Just put them (the patients) in God's hands". He then continued to speak to some of the devotees.

Towards the end I wanted to make the most of the interview, so I waited for another pause and sought Baba's permission to ask something more. I mentioned that we were to have a celebration for His 70th birthday on our return to England. I had also given him an invitation from Mr. Patel. Baba immediately answered, "I know, I know". I asked, "Could you please give me one of your robes to be put on your chair for the celebration?" To my amazement Baba got up from His chair, smiling and looking straight at me, put His hands at His sides and said, "Why do you want my robe – take me!" Everybody in the room burst out laughing. What He said took me by surprise and in my excitement I opened my arms and said to Him, "Oh Baba, yes, I'll take You, please come with me". I was putting my hands together begging Him to come with me. Baba looked very amused by it all, and, on this note the interview came to an end, everyone having had a good laugh. He walked to the door and said to everybody, "I will see you again individually".

But we did not have another interview. We gathered Baba did not necessarily mean He would see us during this trip. It could be at a time known only to Him. He would know the right time and place. As Baba stood next to me on His way to the door, I caught a whiff of the most beautiful fragrance emanating from Him, a blend of roses and jasmine. This was the first time I had smelled such a heavenly fragrance, as I did not notice it before when Baba was close to me and put His hand on my head at the beginning of the interview.

As we walked back to take our place for the remainder of the Bhajans, I cupped my hands together, wondering whether I could still smell any of Baba's Divine fragrance, since I had touched Baba's feet, His hand, and laid my hands on His cushion. I wanted to recapture His presence through His fragrance. As I breathed from my cupped hands, I was transported into ecstasy, as I smelled His Divine fragrance again, of roses and jasmine. I kept taking deep breaths, filling my lungs with it continuously while the Bhajans were taking place.

The lady on my right noticed what I was doing and leaned over to smell my hands. She too could smell the fragrance and exclaimed, "Oh how lucky you are". When we got up after the Bhajans people must have noticed and came to ask if they could smell my hands, sharing in Baba's act of Grace.

I felt I had to be by myself to take it all in and remain with this feeling of joy for as long as I could. I did not feel that I wanted to talk to anyone. But I was not left alone. Everyone came to me, talking to me, wanting to know what had happened in the interview room. The fragrance stayed with me until the evening. I felt that I did not wish to wash my hands or have a bath, nor even to eat, but I was hungry and dusty at the end of the day and went to the canteen after all for a meal. I returned to my shed, had a shower, and went to bed feeling so grateful for Baba's blessings.

I had had the greatest of all privileges in this one interview. I got everything I dreamed of. I wished for Baba to put His hand over my head. This He did, twice. He gave me His blessing verbally. I had a great desire to kiss His hand. He let me do that, again twice. I wanted to kiss His feet, which I did. I talked to Him and He looked at me. I felt such closeness to Him, as never before, such contentment and peace, that, if I had nothing more, I had been granted all I had wished for in that one interview. I can only say that our entire group were on 'cloud nine'. We felt so blessed and so unbelievably elated and filled with joy. Our cup of happiness was full to overflowing.

This is perhaps the place to mention the so-called 'miracles'. People ask, "Why does He do them?" Baba says they give confidence to devotees, help them to retain contact, and is a symbol of His love for them. Other people cynically say that any clever magician could do the same. That is plausible only to those who have never observed Baba.

I have seen so much produced over the years, so many articles created, close to me, that there is not the slightest chance of deception, and I am just one among hundreds of thousands who have seen the same. And, in any event, unlike the magician, Baba gives away everything He creates, from the vibhuthi ash to precious jewels. There is no deception. It is all honest, real and wonderful. Yet the greatest miracle is the positive transformation of those who come to Him.

The more important question is how this reality is created, seemingly out of nothing. This takes us into the realm of modern science, of diagnosis and therapies linked to homeopathy, spiritual healing, and radionics, and above all to the immense power of thought forces possessed by a few special people.

Thought is a frequency. Material items are all frequencies. By thought a material item can be created, as seen by people like Sai Baba, Jesus, and Moses. I believe this century will see a new revelation of the power of these thought forces, so incredibly illustrated by Baba's story.

Chapter 13

BABA ACKNOWLEDGES THE BOOK

There are no unnatural or supernatural phenomena, only very large gaps in our knowledge of what is natural. We should strive to fill these gaps of ignorance.

Edgar Mitchell, Apollo 14 Astronaut

On the 9th October 1995, two weeks before leaving for my fifth trip to 'Prasanthi Nilayam', I woke up at home having remembered vividly every detail of the following dream, something which rarely happens. Usually I only remember fragments of my dreams and am not always able to interpret them.

In my dream, I walked into a narrow room. Facing me on the wall hung a large photograph of Baba covered in vibhuti. I knew that there was going to be a Bhajans in my friend Dulcie's house, but the place did not look like Dulcie's home. There was so much vibhuti all over and around the photograph. At each corner of the photograph were large lacy cobwebs through which I could see thick blobs of vibhuti. (I recognised the photograph from Mr. Patel's temple although it did not have cobwebs as the one in my dream).

I asked Dulcie, "How did you get the photograph transported?" I was surprised that all the vibhuti was intact after being moved from Mr. Patel's Temple, as Dulcie told me that Mr. Patel had lent her the photograph for the Bhajans. I looked to my right and saw a door. I walked through it into a large hall with rows of chairs as if arranged for a meeting or conference. There was an aisle between the rows of chairs. Baba was standing in front of the first row in the aisle. I walked in and took my seat in the first row leaving the chair nearest to Baba for Dulcie, as I knew she was somewhere in the hall and would soon come in. There were no other people in the hall. I was the only one there, as all the seats around me were empty.

Baba turned to me saying, "Where is the...book?" I didn't catch the missing word He had mentioned. I looked around to see if I could find the book. Suddenly I noticed Dulcie's handbag on her chair. I looked inside it in case she had the book, but it was not there. I looked again anxiously all around me and under the chairs, but there was no sign of the book. Somewhat downhearted I turned to Baba saying, "I can't find the book". At this moment Dulcie came and I was surprised that instead of sitting on the chair I had left for her, nearest Baba, she somehow swapped chairs with me, pushing me gently into her chair! I found myself sitting very close to Baba, His right arm almost touching me, so I laid my head on His arm saying to Him softly "Baba, I love you". He smiled at me, then pulled His arm gently away, at which point I woke up.

Next morning, I went to meet my friend Marguerite as we were working together on this book. On hearing about my dream she told me to write it all down while fresh in my mind, which I did. Everything was so clear and vivid to me. That evening, I went to Mr. Patel's Temple for Arathi (ceremony of light). On entering the Temple, one of the ladies led me to the photograph I had brought from Puttaparthi for Baba's 68th birthday, which He had signed 'With Love, Baba'. She said to me, "Look at your picture". When I looked I was astonished to see white vibhuti dotted over Baba's hair, looking exactly like the lace I saw in my dream. There was also a thick mass of vibhuti in the middle of his forehead between His eyebrows, the area where the 'third eye' is located (Picture 11). The vibhuti also reminded me of the blobs I had seen in my dream. And all this vibhuti appeared in Mr. Patel's Temple the day after my dream!

The following Thursday (Baba's special day), I came to the Temple. There was yet another manifestation of vibhuti on the same picture. One of Mr. Patel's close friends drew my attention to the space below the signature where a large heart in white vibhuti had now appeared. I was astonished, puzzled, but elated. Marguerite, who was with me, said, "That must be Baba's response to your saying to Him 'I love you' in the dream. She felt that with the appearance of this heart He was saying, "I love you too". The timing of these manifestations was extraordinary, coming straight after my dream. Baba says that no one dreams of Him unless He wills it, so my dream came from Him as a message, which I interpret as follows:

Cobwebs signify the passage of time, undisturbed, old, stored-up memories and experiences in the sub-conscious, which I had to bring to the surface. At the start of writing I was concerned whether I would be able to remember all the incidents of long ago, as well as how to express them. The dream came to reassure me that, as I saw through the cobwebs of the vibhuti, in the same way I would awaken and find the spiritual essence from all these experiences to record in my book. In the dream I was puzzled about vibhuti remaining on the picture after being moved from one house to another. This was to prove that with God's help anything could be achieved. By saying, "Where is the book?" Baba was encouraging me to carry on with the book, and with His help, clear up the cobwebs. This is my interpretation of the interplay of my dream and real life.

On 28th October 1995, two weeks after the dream, I was once again bound for 'Prasanthi Nilayam', Baba's ashram. It was to be Baba's 70th Birthday celebration year. I should explain that, although born in 1926, He is regarded as one year old at birth. After arrival we speedily settled in and got organised before the multitude of people began to arrive.

On the 9th November we lined up as usual for Darshan. Word was passed round that Baba would see us! We could not believe this, as we had not yet received our row number. We heard another rumour that Baba would see all Western groups. We could not understand, as there were so many of us, comprising more than a thousand people. When finally we were in the Mandir area, we were told to sit back to back in rows facing each other leaving a space in between, which we guessed must be to enable Baba to walk between the rows. We were excited at this opportunity to have Him come so close to us, giving us the chance to give Him our letters and items to bless.

After some time music began to play (the usual sign that Baba had come out of His residence). We saw Baba emerge through the gate. He had a happy smile on His face. Six Seva Dal ladies were hurrying towards Him, their arms loaded with saris. We assumed these saris were for His students, or their teachers, as we have seen Him distribute saris to them on many occasions. However, we were in for a great surprise.

As Baba came across to us, He began to walk between our lines, giving with His own hands a sari to each of us. We had the opportunity to touch His gown or His Lotus Feet, which I promptly did when He came in front of me. He dropped the sari into my waiting hands, looking at me with a beautiful smile and an expression of joy in giving us such a surprise, like a father giving unexpected gifts to His children. I was so moved. Tears rolled down my face. I looked around. There were not many dry eyes to be seen. We were all overwhelmed by Baba's love and generosity, but that was not all. We learned later from an Italian group who had an interview with Baba that He told them the saris had healing vibrations and that if ever anyone felt unwell they should cover themselves with the sari.

Afterwards trays were brought to the veranda by a few of the college boys who are always at hand to help. At least a hundred Indian ladies who, I was later told, were workers within various service organisations of Baba's such as teachers, nurses, volunteers were called by some Seva Dals to come to the front of the Mandir grounds and sit in lines. The trays contained watches, which Baba dropped into the hands or lap of each of these ladies, who prostrated themselves at His feet, kissing or touching His robe with reverence and gratitude. What a moving sight it was!

Baba then gave the college boys watches in a presentation box, but did not distribute them Himself as He had done with the ladies, but instead asked His closest aides to do so. The young lads at first protested and refused to accept the gift unless given by Baba, but later relented, as no doubt they realised that they had Baba's attention throughout the year, and so they accepted the watches with gratitude. Baba is always involved in guiding and encouraging them individually, in their academic careers, and in character- building from primary school to post-graduate level.

It was an afternoon to remember, to cherish. We got up, each one of us clutching the sari to our heart, happy beyond words and so grateful. The great bonus was that while He was giving us the saris individually, each of us had a private Darshan of our beloved Baba. What more could we ask?

On 11th November, we drew row number two. I felt I might be able to give Baba the first part of my manuscript, which I hoped He would bless. However, when He came out, He passed us by, taking letters instead from the opposite side to us. It seemed another chance had been missed. Was it not yet the right time to bless my manuscript? After Darshan, some people left for breakfast, but I stayed. I was lucky to be able to move forward to the first line as soon as someone got up and left. I sat down and tried to pass the long hour until Bhajans began by reading.

After Bhajans, on returning to His residence Baba came close to me. I lifted my manuscript up asking Him to bless it. He looked at me and gently made a sign with His hand, saying "Wait, wait. later, later", while looking at me and then at the cover of the manuscript which had the title printed on it. From His look, I could see that He knew all about the manuscript. What He meant by these words, I would find out in time. At least I felt that it was something positive and that I should continue with my writing, tuning into His guidance.

During the last few days of our visit, crowds had poured continuously into the ashram in preparation for Baba's 70th birthday celebration. Queues grew longer and longer for Darshans and Bhajans, as well as at the canteen for meals. The next day, miraculously, we drew row number one, and excitedly we hurried into the Mandir grounds. We would have a good view of Baba when He would emerge.

We prayed and hoped for an interview. Baba came out, gliding slowly and gracefully as He approached in our direction, while taking letters here and there, having a word or two with a few lucky devotees. As He passed us, Nancy, a member of our group, asked Him for an interview. Baba asked her "How many?" she answered "seventeen", and He continued to walk. I then saw Him stop by an American devotee asking her "How many?" She answered, "Fourteen" and I heard him say the magic word "Go!" The young lady jumped up with a great big smile on her face and hurried to the veranda of the Mandir, the rest of her group following her.

As Baba continued walking towards us, I held up my book with a letter, praying He would take the letter and bless the manuscript. Alison, a member of our group, also held a Bhajan book, which she had compiled and wanted Baba to bless, but He just passed by and our hearts sank in disappointment. We were so near, yet so far, but realised that Baba gives us what we need when the time is right and not before. We should accept with equanimity whatever happens. This is what He is trying to teach us. All these are tests and we must pass our grade however difficult.

At the end of Darshan Baba distributed more saris and watches to the teachers and others working at the colleges. All the several thousands assembled received Indian sweets from Baba's lady volunteers. Baba is always happy just giving, never receiving. On the occasion of this 70th birthday Baba unveiled the completion of a water project whereby 700 villages were provided with clean running water. Previously, villagers had to walk many miles only to get dirty and polluted water. He also distributed 70 sewing machines, 70 bicycles adapted to physically disabled children and adults, and conducted 70 weddings, providing the required clothing and jewellery for the brides and bridegrooms as well as free food and soft drinks for them and their guests.

The next day our group decided to meet a little earlier as the crowds were increasing all the time. It was expected there would be about one-and-a-half million people coming for Baba's 70th birthday. Preparations to accommodate this multitude and also to feed every one of them were underway. Baba let it be known that all accommodation and food were to be provided free of charge during the week. It was nothing short of a miracle to watch as new dormitories, sinks and taps, new toilets; two new canteens were completed within two weeks.

Marquees were set up everywhere to give shade from the scorching sun. Decorated arches were erected covered in garlands, flags and spiritual symbols. In every corner coloured lights were placed and there were numerous bookstalls selling books in all languages. There were also information centres, telephones and fax stalls. Everyday as we awoke, something new had sprung up to make people as comfortable as possible for the celebrations. It was truly a Herculean task, but always done with love and dedication. Baba took a great personal interest in every stage of the construction, driving around, meeting the workers, talking to them and blessing them.

A new and beautiful canteen was completed during the two weeks while we were in the ashram, with splendid marble columns and stairs. At the entrance to the canteen hung separate life-sized photographs of Shirdi Baba and of Sai Baba decorated with garlands, ready for Baba's blessings at the opening ceremony of the canteen. The beauty of the Mandir decorations is difficult to describe, truly works of art and labours of love. Coloured lights were strung around the balcony and walls of the Mandir. The columns were decorated with lacy garlands and colourful flags. It was all breathtakingly beautiful – a fairytale sight. Volunteers put up the decorations in a miraculously short time, working throughout the night with love and joy. We were not allowed to take photographs, but videotapes of the birthday celebration have since been released.

Baba leaves one in awe by His inexhaustible energy and generosity. He is always giving. On the 23rd of November 1995, His 70th Birthday, It was reported that one and a half million devotees attended the celebration. All of them were fed three meals a day free for a whole week. The food never ran out! Food for this entire multitude for a whole week, in our Western eyes is unbelievable, but in Baba's Presence, a simple fact of reality!

A further visit – 1996

I made yet another a trip to Baba a year later on October 30th 1996. This time I made no notes in my diary, as the weather was so hot and humid, more than I have experienced in the past. Perspiration literally ran down my back and face, sapping my energy, so I put off writing from day to day. However memories of my trip remain.

We were a group of sixteen – twelve ladies, four men. As usual we met at Heathrow Airport. The flight was not only on time, which was surprising, but in fact we were called about twenty minutes early! A smooth flight to Bombay, and thence to Bangalore. Everything went according to schedule. After resting at Bangalore, taxis took us to Puttaparthi, where we were lucky to get rooms in a newly built block of flats. Everything was new and functioning. What a relief! There were just three of us in our room, my friend Dalia, myself, and an elderly Indian lady.

A week after our arrival, on Wednesday 6th November 1996, to our great surprise and joy, we were thrilled to be called for an interview. We sat on the Mandir balcony, happiness written on all our faces. Before leaving for India, I had been in two minds whether to take the manuscript of my book with me, as I had not yet finished writing it. However, my dear friend Marguerite (who travelled with us) suggested that I should take the manuscript for Baba's blessings. I was so glad I listened to her.

Carole, our group leader, brought with her the two manuals about Baba's Education in Human Values, which she had compiled so beautifully. This is a curriculum for the development of character, which has been adopted by many schools. To date, in at least 80 schools in the UK and in many more schools around the world, the EHV program has transformed children, with an astonishing effect on their schoolwork, behaviour and relationships; a vast beneficial transformation, and a hope for a better future society. I present here a few of Carole's own words about the programme, taken from one of the manuals:

> *"The programme is a simple and structured method of developing positive values in young people. It is based on values, which have underpinned the noble thoughts and achievements of mankind throughout history and are an inherent part in the human personality. There will be other aspects of education, which also contribute to social, moral, spiritual and cultural education in children aged six to sixteen years.*
>
> *The programme is international and is being developed and culturally adapted for use in countries as far apart as the USA, Canada, Europe, India, Thailand, Malaysia and Australia. Its popularity is spreading rapidly throughout the world. In summer 1995, Mr. Frederico Mayor, Director*

> *General of UNESCO, visited Sathya Sai in Bangalore and wished the Sathya Sai Institute success in its implementation of the Programme which would further the cause of world peace through education. He looked forward to establishing close links with them."*

When one is in Baba's presence and He looks at you, there is that feeling that He looks through you into your inner being, not the outer form. He constantly proves that He knows the past, present, and future of everyone, all our thoughts and desires. Nothing can be hidden from Him. Frequently Baba would answer devotees' questions even before they had asked them. He also told people their dreams in detail. He did this to Louise, one of the ladies in our group during the interview, much to her amazement. Baba says that when one dreams of Him, it is because of His will to come to this person to guide or give comfort, according to the need.

When Baba called us in, we sat around Him. Carole, Dalia and I sat close to His chair. The first thing He did was to manifest white vibhuti for the ladies. He then sat down. Carole presented the manual to Baba, which He opened, looked at, and seemed very pleased with. He patted Carole on her head, saying "Good girl". Carole's face was radiant with happiness. Baba then looked at me, so I gave Him my manuscript, saying, "I am writing a book but I have not finished it yet, should I continue?" He took the manuscript from my hand and put it on His lap, looked at a few pages, and said, "Yes, finish it", handing the manuscript back to me. I was delighted and grateful to have Baba's approval and encouragement.

The interview lasted about 40 minutes; Baba then distributed packets of vibhuti to each of us. We left the interview room happy and blessed, especially since this was, for a number of devotees, their first interview. They were overjoyed. Carole was especially thrilled as Baba manifested for her a long golden chain, with 108 knots, which he told her never to take off as it was for her protection.

On our last day and our last Darshan, we had the unexpected surprise of an unusual and delightful spectacle. It was a special festival of one of the Hindu Deities. There was to be a procession led by Baba's pet elephant, Sai Gita. As the gates opened Sai Gita entered the Mandir grounds resplendent in exquisite regalia. She walked in slowly and proudly, full of majesty and with well-disciplined grace. As we sat quite near we had a good view. We were elated at being able to see the procession as a final treat before returning home.

A few minutes after Sai Gita entered the Mandir grounds, Baba walked slowly towards his beloved elephant. When Sai Gita saw Baba she had to be held back from running toward Him. Baba stroked her trunk and Sai Gita showed her love for her master by wrapping her trunk around Him. It was so moving to see the love between them. When Baba walked away from Sai Gita, she pulled her handler, wanting to follow Baba, but was held back. She looked sad and downhearted when Baba left. One of the ladies, sitting close by, commented that she could see tears coming from Sai Gita's eyes! And so we left Puttaparthi to return home to England, filled with joy and happy memories.

I was by now a confirmed devotee of Sai Baba, the ship of my life having finally arrived and dropped anchor at the safe harbour of His Divine teaching. His are the Universal Truths taught by all religions and expounded by prophets and saints throughout human existence, of which the Ten Commandments are the foundation. Baba teaches the highest moral and ethical values, which are saturated with the nectar of His pure love. One cannot help but be touched and transformed by it. Sai Baba has come at this crucial time to re-assert these truths and to teach us by His own example, showing us how to live by actively putting these commandments into our daily lives.

Thus we find the "peace that passeth all understanding", happiness and contentment, in spite of the knocks and stresses of our life's journey. Baba puts great emphasis on love and selfless service. From love springs all the other virtues without which we could never find the endlessly sought-after peace and happiness. He always emphasises "My Life is My Message", and truly He is the embodiment of universal love, peace, selfless service, and pure bliss. How fortunate and blessed are we who have found such a teacher.

Chapter 14

THE COCONUT

*If you have secured the Grace of God,
you are reinforced with so much strength that you
can carry out the most difficult tasks.*

Sathya Sai Baba

My story would not be complete without describing yet another incident which occurred on Friday evening the 6th June 1997. It occurred during the monthly Bhajans at Mr. Patel's temple, a week after completing most of this book.

Thursday 22nd May was the ninth anniversary since Baba's first 'visit' to Mr. Patel's home. As most devotees know, Baba always explains that number nine, or any numbers adding up to nine, are, for astrological reasons, lucky, auspicious. On that day, a special Bhajans was organised and the Temple decorated as always with a beautiful fresh flower arrangements. There was also an exquisite flower arrangement forming the number '9' in sky blue, white and orange petals.

Nine coconuts were placed in the temple in front of a large photograph of Baba that was totally covered in vibhuti. Each coconut had a different symbol of a religion on it, depicted in red. Four coconuts together spelled the word L-O-V-E. The remaining coconuts had the first letter of Baba's five human values. All nine coconuts were blessed with vibhuti on that day, and amazingly they all had an identical horizontal hairline crack on them. Also, on Baba's chair was a large sign of 'Om' in vibhuti. On Baba's foot-rest, over some flowers that were placed there, one could see the figure eight in vibhuti (number eight is Mr. Patel's house number).

As we entered Mr. Patel's house on Friday 6th June 1997, which was the usual monthly Bhajans day, each of us were asked to pick a small folded piece of paper from a box. If it had a number on it we were to keep it, if not, we were to drop it into another box. I unfolded my piece of paper, which revealed the number 'five', so I slipped it into my pocket. No one had any idea what these numbers were for. The Temple area filled up to capacity. Those who could not get into the Temple area sat on blankets in the kitchen, the dining room, and the lounge. There must have been at least 120 people in the house for the Bhajans.

When the Bhajans ended and following the Arathi ceremony, it was announced that whoever had picked a number was to be given one of the cracked coconuts that were also blessed with vibhuti, a lucky and auspicious gift. I counted the coconuts from left to right and mine was the fifth one, since I had picked number five. This coconut depicted a sign of the Jewish religion, with the Star of David drawn in red glitter! (Picture 12) My heart started pounding, I could not believe my eyes.

How amazing and unbelievable! I was the only Jewish person at this particular Bhajans, though there are sometimes one or two Jewish devotees, but they had not come on this occasion.

I gave my piece of paper to Mini (Mr. Patel's daughter), who picked up the fifth coconut and, smiling, she handed it to me. She looked as surprised as I was, as were all the people who knew me. I cannot put into words how I felt. Out of about 109 tickets with only nine numbers and 100 blanks, the chances of this happening are only one in 109, and that I should pick up the one depicting my religion was nothing short of a miracle. A friend said that Baba might have been acknowledging the completion of my book with His special grace. I hoped she was right.

I left the Temple charged with so much love and energy, hugging everyone near me, holding my treasured prize close to my heart. When I arrived home, I was so overwhelmed with joy that I could not fall asleep until the early hours of the morning. As I was one of the last to leave the Temple, Mr. Patel told me that he too was graced with Baba's blessings, and said that an unopened ticket for one of the coconuts was left for him, and therefore remained in the Temple! How perfectly Baba works His plans. My gratitude knew no bounds. Indeed, out of my bitter experience over so many years had come the sweetness of God's Grace and Love.

The Symbolic Meaning of the Coconut

Hindus believe that the coconut is the purest form of offering one can tender to God. The fruit is unique in many respects.

The sweet nectar, like the water that it holds, is pure and untouched by human hands. The tree draws it from its very base to its highest level.

Symbolically, the coarsely-knit outer fibres of the coconut represent the jealousy, greed, lust, selfishness and other vices of man, which must be removed, and the shell broken before it can be penetrated. One can then reach the white inner purity and thereafter taste the sweet untouched nectar of spiritual purity and bliss.

No other fruit has the three distinct eyes of the coconut. These symbolise the Trinity of Creation, Preservation and Dissolution.

The eyes also represent the three eyes of man, the two physical eyes plus the third inner eye, the eye of super-consciousness. Only this inner eye can penetrate the false façade and reach the Ultimate Truth, which distinguishes right from wrong.

The composition of the coconut is characteristic of the three elements of man. This hard, outer shell, with its coarse fibres represent man's physiological element and the untouched water signifies his spiritual composition.

Having been offered to God by way of prayer, the coconut is then eaten by the people as blessed 'prasad' in the belief that it has received divine vibrations and is blessed by God. It will therefore give them good health and prosperity.

The coconut, with its rough exterior and its inner sweetness, in a strange way typified my own journey through life. Looking back, I realised that always close to me, and within me, there existed an unseen, yet strongly felt, helper, indeed a very special Guide. He was always there, protecting inspiring and comforting me whenever I was in need, during crisis or in danger. I now know that all these so-called 'coincidences' were inner guidance, which I received as a response to my cry for help. As a result I have found peace and security beyond the material in the knowledge that indeed we are never alone and abandoned. If we but knock, the door will be opened, and if we seek, we shall find. I have totally surrendered myself to this higher wisdom, this Divine Presence, knowing that it will be with me till the journey's sweet end.

Chapter 15

WITH BABA - EXPECT THE UNEXPECTED

The life of Sai, the messages of Sai, the ideals Sai holds forth, the lessons that Sai teaches the world, are all enshrined in one word – LOVE.

Sathya Sai Baba

The Ring and the Robe

The blessings received from Baba on 2nd November 1997 was a grace I certainly did not expect and for which I am deeply grateful. Once again, another year, another trip, I was on my way to Baba's ashram, my seventh trip.

During my interview in 1996, I presented Baba with my manuscript, two thirds completed. He said to me "Finish it". With His blessings and timely help this had been achieved.

We set off from Heathrow, arriving at the ashram on Friday 31st October 1997 at lunchtime. We had our first Darshan that afternoon. I carried my heavy manuscript to each Darshan and Bhajans hoping that Baba would bless it. My friend Dalia said as we were going to Darshan on Sunday afternoon: "I have a feeling Baba will call us for an interview pretty soon as

I'm sure He won't let you carry this heavy manuscript for long". I said I hoped her feelings would prove right. Indeed on that Sunday 2nd November 1997, at the same Darshan, we were bowled over with surprise and delight when we were called for an interview barely two days after our arrival.

Having finished giving Darshan to thousands of devotees, Baba came to the veranda of the Mandir where we were waiting for Him. As usual He is always the last to come into the room. He makes sure that we are all settled down. Dalia and I sat by Baba's chair. We always seemed to end up there and never miss the opportunity and privilege to touch His Lotus feet. When Baba came in He asked us if we were feeling hot and switched on the fan saying, "Now you will be more comfortable". He then did the now familiar turn of His right hand and produced white vibhuti, which He poured into the palm of the hands of each lady. There was always enough for as many ladies as were present. Gratefully, we ate this holy ash, which is a blessing. For some reason known only to Baba, men do not get this special vibhuti in the interview room.

Together with our group, Baba also called a father and his young son who was six or seven years old. I learned later that they were from Greece. Baba named the boy 'Jay' when he was brought to Him as a baby. He told the father to bring him to His school when he was six years old. The boy had become a student in Baba's school.

Baba sat down on His chair and looked at all of us. He then turned His attention to Jay and asked him, "What do you want?"

Little Jay answered without hesitation, "I want you Baba", to which Baba, half smiling, responded, "Who taught you to say that?" Jay smiled shyly and answered, "No one". Baba then made one circle with His hand and manifested a shiny gold ring with an OM sign on it. He showed it to everyone by holding it up between His thumb and forefinger. He then called Jay to Him and put the ring on his little finger – a perfect fit.

After a short moment Baba looked at little Jay again and said, "Would you rather have a ring with a nice stone?" He took back the ring, held it once again between His thumb and index finger and, without a move, just blew once on the ring. Amazingly, as always, the ring changed to a gold band with a dazzling green stone on it. As I sat at His feet Baba gave me the ring to examine, His 'latest creation', whilst saying to the little boy, "I give to 'grandmother' to see". Little Jay came forward and Baba placed the ring on His finger, which again was a perfect fit.

Without further ado, Baba made another circular movement of His hand and manifested a beautiful silver ring with the image of Shirdi Sai Baba embossed on it. He called Manubhai Patel – our group leader, and placed it on his finger. Manubhai, who had lost a ring Baba had given him a few years earlier, was overcome with joy.

I then took the opportunity of a moment's pause and said, "Baba, you told me last year to finish writing the book and I have now finished it", handing Him the manuscript. Baba put it on His lap and, looking at the title, read it out slowly 'From

Bitter Game Sweet'. I corrected Baba, saying: "Baba, it is came sweet", which I repeated twice. He smiled as He was teasing me or making a point, but as I have come to learn, there is always a meaning and a purpose in whatever Baba says. He lets us work out for ourselves what the message is behind the words. On reflection, I likened Baba's comments to one of His quotes, "Life is a Game – Play It. Life is a Dream – Realise It. Life is a Challenge – Meet It. Life is Love - Enjoy It".

He continued to read out 'My Journey to the Abode of Supreme Peace'. He looked at me, saying, "Why supreme peace? There is nothing higher than peace". He continued looking at some pages and seemed to be reading a few lines here and there and said, "Very happy, very happy". After Baba closed the book, I asked Him, "Please Baba, would you sign it". He answered, "Later", and handed me back the book. I promptly asked Him, "Shall I publish it?" His answer came quickly, "Yes, publish".

Baba then turned to Eileen, one of the ladies in our group, who was sitting at the back, and asked "How are you?" Eileen replied that she was all right. Baba then asked: "Have you got holes in your ears?" (Meaning did she have pierced ears for earrings). Eileen did not answer straight away. Baba repeated his question and Eileen replied, "Yes Swami, I have holes in my ears". Baba then looked at Eileen, asking in a questioning tone, "No earrings?" Eileen answered, "No Swami, no earrings". Baba promptly said, "Would you like earrings?" Eileen answered without hesitation, "Yes, I'd love it, Swami".

He turned His attention to me, asking "Would you like a ring like the little boy?" I said, "Yes please, Baba". So with a swift turn of His right hand he manifested a shimmering gold ring with an OM sign engraved on it (Picture 13), which He placed on the second finger of my right hand. I kissed His Divine hand, saying "Thank you, Baba". The ring was a perfect fit. I suddenly heard myself say, "Baba, I love you", to which He replied sweetly, "I love you too". At that moment when I said these words to Him it seemed that I was alone with Baba, and that there was no one around. I totally forgot my surroundings for that brief moment.

Baba called our small group into His private interview room. He spoke to some of the people about personal matters, always astonishing us with His knowledge of every detail of our lives. We returned to the main room and waited until Baba had finished speaking in private to Jay and his father and to the other couples in turn.

When we were all back in the main room, Baba sat in His chair and turned His attention once again to Eileen. He said to her, "Your health is good, but you need to lose weight. It is bad for your heart". He continued saying to her, "Too much worry, too much hurry, too much curry!" We all laughed as Eileen nodded her head, agreeing with Baba. (We learned later how true this was with regard to her life).

He said to Eileen, "What do you want?" To which Eileen replied somewhat cheekily, "I want you Baba, and my earrings!" Baba immediately obliged, making the familiar movement with His right hand palm down, and, turning His palm up, I could clearly see two glistening gold drop earrings which He put into my hand, saying to me, "You put them on her", calling Eileen to come forward. I looked at the beautiful earrings, ornately carved and fashioned. With them were also two plastic butterfly fastenings.

As Eileen came to sit near me, I was in a dilemma. I was worried that I might not be able to find the holes in her earlobes. My spectacles were in my bag and I did not want to hold everyone up while I searched for them, so I decided to give it a try. I took hold of Eileen's earlobe and looked for the hole to insert the loop of the earring, but to my dismay I could not see it. I was afraid that if I took a chance and inserted it into the wrong place, Eileen would give a shriek and how embarrassing that would be. How could I face Baba? So I gave Eileen the earrings and told her, "You put them on, as I don't want to hurt you". She promptly did so, her face glowing with happiness, tears filling her eyes.

Baba rose and went through a curtained door. From a previous interview, I remembered that He came out from behind the curtain with a robe identical to the one He Himself wears. The thought flashed through my mind, Baba is going to give someone a robe. Indeed, within a second He appeared holding one of His orange robes. He looked at me as I looked at Him.

Before I realised it, He tossed the robe from about eight feet away over the heads of some of the devotees, and to my utter shock, surprise and joy, the robe landed perfectly folded on my lap as if it had been carefully placed there!

I clutched it to my chest and, as I hugged the robe with both my hands, I felt warm vibrations and energy penetrating my entire being. It was such a soothing and comforting feeling. I do not know how I did not break down in sobs, as the blessing I had received overwhelmed me. I know Baba does not like to see us cry. Maybe He helped me to control myself. However, many tears of gratitude have been shed since.

Baba asked someone to bring Him a red basket, which was on the windowsill. In it He keeps packets of vibhuti. He distributed to each of us a handful of the packets to take home with us. Then He opened the door and walked onto the veranda. We followed Him out of the room, all of us deeply moved, and infinitely grateful for an unforgettable experience, especially for those for whom this was their first interview. I walked out clutching the robe and my book against my chest. As we sat down for the Bhajans, I placed the robe safely into the cellophane bag in which I had my manuscript, and then into a plastic bag. Later Eileen related to us the reason for Baba giving her the earrings.

Apparently, her friend Janet had decided to come to Puttaparthi in October and had asked Eileen to come with her. However, Eileen told Janet that she had too many problems and that on top of it all, she also had to move house and had no money for the trip. Janet would not take no for an answer and carried on, insisting that Eileen should come with her. Finally Eileen decided that the only way she could manage to go would be to pawn her best earrings and a brooch, which raised enough money for the trip.

No wonder Baba had asked her, "No earrings? Do you want earrings?" Once again Baba proved to doubters that He knows everything about what we think, what we do, no matter where we are. After the gift of earrings, Eileen could not stop crying on and off for two days. She walked about in a daze, deeply touched by Baba's thoughtfulness and Grace. It more than compensated for all her recent troubles.

That evening, blessed with the robe and the ring, I went to bed happy and grateful. I tried to sleep, but was wide-awake with excitement. It was then that I experienced a pain in my chest, which was getting gradually stronger, but I thought that it would probably soon go away. I put my hand on my heart, giving myself healing, but the pain did not subside. I waited for 15 or 20 minutes, wondering what it could be.

I feared it might perhaps be the first signs of a heart attack or a stroke, so I finally woke my friend Dalia, telling her how I felt. She came over and gave me healing. Her hands were very hot, but the pain did not lessen. Our third roommate, Conchita, then said, "Ruth, put the robe Baba gave you on your body". Conchita took the robe and placed it over me.

Once again I felt its warm vibration. Almost instantly, the pain ceased and never returned!

What a journey I had had and what an experience, Baba's blessing for my book, the beautiful gold ring, and His precious robe. I was filled with joy, and the desire to dedicate my every thought, word and deed to serve and be worthy of His love and blessings.

Shanti Shanti Shanti

ॐ

Peace Peace Peace

PART THREE

INTRODUCTION

Thus have I related my story. Some, who have had similar experiences, will accept the truth of what I have set down. Others, especially those to whom the story of Sai Baba is new, may be more sceptical. They have not perceived the reality of Baba, but only my written word about Him. They may think that here is a woman who has become obsessed with an idealised figure, from whatever impulses, whatever motives, whatever needs.

If it were I alone, that attitude might be understandable. But thousands upon thousands of men and women, of all ages, religions, nationalities and occupations, have independently reacted to Baba in the same way as I have. I would urge those who remain cynical or unconvinced to read the books mentioned in the Appendix and study Baba's sayings in this last part of the book.

Baba has no wish to establish a new religion. He wishes each person to look more deeply into his or her own faith, but to look also for the basic unity behind that diversity. I have followed that advice and have looked more deeply into my own Jewish inheritance. That search is included in this part of my story.

Through Baba's inspiration I have learned much of my own tradition I had never previously known. This may apply to you, whatever your background, whatever your beliefs. As Baba urges, "Come, test, inquire, taste, experience."

THOUGHTS AND PRAYERS

In all humility I relay the inspirational thoughts and prayers that have come to me in meditation. I do not claim to be their author. I am only a channel through which these messages have come to bring love, light and hope.

To the Lord I have dedicated
my voice, my eyes, my hands,
my heart, my body, my feelings
my will – my being.

ॐ

May I soar on the wings
of faith to my home in Thee.

ॐ

Oh my Beloved, my heart mind and soul
I place on the altar of my love for Thee.

ॐ

Divine Mother, illuminate my heart with Thy Love
my mind with Thy wisdom,
my soul with Thy peace.

ॐ

Let me dig ever deeper
with the axe of determination
into the depths of my soul,
where I shall unite and dwell in Thee.

ॐ

Oh God, awaken Thy children from ignorance
that they may discover Thee.

ॐ

My Divine Mother
ignite the ember of my love
for Thee that it may forever burn fed
with the logs of my devotion.

ॐ

May the prayers of gratitude of Thy children
who have been healed be a silent testimony
of my devoted service to Thee
May I always be Thy humble instrument

ॐ

Live in an attitude of gratitude, why worry – everything comes from God and everything belongs to God. We have brought nothing with us when we were born so why not be grateful for what we have received. If we deserve more, God will provide.

ॐ

May all my desires be burnt
in the fire of my Love for Thee.

ॐ

Oh Divine Mother
Help me to accept and endure
with the right attitude whatever condition I may have
knowing that it is for my ultimate good
and that through these tests I come ever
closer to Thee in Self Realisation.

ॐ

All knowledge is in the ether – all inventions, inspirations are picked up through concentration or attunement to the all-knowing intelligence in the ether. Like a radio or television, the mind needs to be on the right wavelength to pick it up.

ॐ

Divine Mother
Whatever tests you put me through

give me the strength
the courage and wisdom
to learn the lessons
they have come to teach me.

ॐ

Divine Father
Lead me from darkness to light
from ignorance to wisdom
from restlessness to peace
from desire to contentment
free me of all obstacles
and lead me
to Thy shore of divine fulfilment.

ॐ

Divine Mother
Illumine my mind with Thy wisdom,
My heart with Thy love,
My body with Thy energy.

ॐ

Ruth Grant

Philosophy from Self Realized Souls:-

Dr. Paul Brunton: A Message from Arunachalla
Published by Rider, London 1977

Blessed is the man who has found his own self.

ॐ

Life refuses to yield its sublime secret to the lazy. If you want to find out its true meaning why then you must begin to look for it. And the place to look is within.

ॐ

We know ourselves as human beings, but we have yet to know ourselves as spiritual beings.

ॐ

How little do we know that which we are!
How less what we may be.

ॐ

After all, the best aristocracy is that of the soul.
A man is great, not because he was born into an exalted rank, but
because he was born with an exalted soul.

ॐ

If only people would let go of everything for a few minutes every day, dropping all tension, relaxing every muscle of the body, reposing the mind and slowing the breath, they might begin to provide the requisite conditions whereby the overself could make its serenity felt throughout their lives. Thus they would daily learn to withdraw quietly into its peace. Nor would their activities really suffer, even though a little time had been stolen from them. For life would become more balanced, duties would be carried out in a calmer and more collected manner, each crisis or emergency would find them both ready and steady, free from panic.

ॐ

Love is the most powerful force in the Universe. That is why the Supreme Being must ultimately conquer the world. For He loves His creatures so much that they will all yield themselves completely to Him one day.

ॐ

In a sense misery is your best friend,
because it starts you seeking God!

Paramahansa Yogananda

ॐ

Finding God is the funeral of all sorrows.

Swami Sri Yukteswar

Happiness – a word very commonly used, a goal very few attain, or the meaning of which only few truthfully know and even fewer can retain

Anon.

ॐ

Higher and nobler than all ordinary ones are another set of teachers – the Avatars of Iswara. They are the teachers of all teachers, the highest manifestation of God in Man

Sage Swami Vivekananda

ॐ

For the Lord has come in order to test you

Moses to the Children of Israel – Exodus

ॐ

Lord, give me strength that I
May give strength to others
Give me health that I may
Give health to others
Give me love that I may
Give love to others
Give me peace that I may
Give peace to others

Aubrey Rose

ॐ

Daily Prayers

May I be thankful for all the Blessings I already have. Grant me relief from pain and sickness, protect me from ills and grant me good health in the days to come. Remove all causes of imperfection and bring Thy Healing Ministers to me that I may be conscious of their presence and so receive guidance and inspiration.

Grant me courage and fortitude to overcome all adversity. Let me be conscious of Thy strength in all times of need. Grant me confidence to overcome my fears and not to anticipate harm. Teach me, how to live rightly in Thy sight, to do only that which is right and true.

I pray that good guidance and right influencing will inspire all Thy people to be as brothers, one to the other, and that peace shall endure for all time". AMEN

Harry Edwards (famous healer)

ॐ

Blessed Lord, Help me to carry light of Thy Divine
Spirit into the world
That I may never cast gloom over any heart.
May Thy holy radiance shine in my face
And find expression through my words and actions

Grant unto me the power to cheer the sad
Comfort the distressed and bring Thy blessings
To all lives that touch my life.

Unknown

ॐ

Prayer to the Lord

O LORD!
Take my heart
and let it flow in fullness of devotion to Thee
Take my love
and let it flow in fullness of devotion to thee
Take my hands
and let them work incessantly for thee

Take my body
and let it be in devotion dedicated to Thee
Take my everything
and let it be an instrument to work for Thee
Take my life
and let it be consecrated for Thee
Take my soul
and let it be merged in one with Thee

Sathya Sai Baba Prayer Book

ॐ

THE RABBI AND THE GURU

"No harm can ever befall a person whose heart is full of compassion, whose words are adorned with truth and whose body is dedicated to the welfare of others."

Sathya Sai Baba

Returning to London after stirring experiences in India, I began to think back over the course my life had taken. Raised within a traditional Jewish family in pre-independence Israel, married at the age of 17, a young innocent, my husband coming from a mixed background. He was Jewish, having a British citizenship because his father was born in Malta. His mother was a Rumanian Jewess and I believe his father had both Rumanian and Austrian origins. My husband, his two brothers and two sisters, were all born, educated and raised in Egypt. We met and married in Israel while he was serving in the Royal Air Force.

We lived in Egypt, Israel, and France, finally settling in England. Life was hard but after many years of struggle my husband's business prospered. This led to a comfortable life, with every material advantage; beautiful home, expensive holidays, designer clothes, and help at home. I could easily have lived out my life, as others do, on a purely materialistic plane, totally unaware of the spiritual potential in and around me.

Then came the accident, which shattered my world, my home, my marriage, and almost ended my life. That tragedy changed something inside me. It made me realise, for the first time, the smallness, and the pettiness, which had surrounded me. It opened my eyes, figuratively and literally, for only one eye now functioned, to a broader vision.

This led me to the ashram in America of the spiritual guru Paramahansa Yogananda. Even my journey from airport to ashram was fraught with danger to my life, which through the grace of God, never materialised.

I learned much from my two visits to Yogananda. Perhaps they prepared me for deeper experiences in Puttaparthi. I began to gain new treasures, of a spiritual kind, at the same time as I lost husband, home and most of the material and financial support I had previously enjoyed. I was now alone. My children also had a difficult time.

Looking back I can see how my family continued to live in a set conventional way, whilst I was venturing far beyond the boundaries of their pattern of life and in a different direction.

In the process of re-evaluating my life, I pondered on my Jewish inheritance, a very rich inheritance. I observed the seeming miracles achieved by Sai Baba and compared them with Biblical accounts.

Baba had fed multitudes with an endless supply of food that seemed to appear from nowhere. So, too, did the prophet Elisha, as also did the teacher, Jesus the Nazarene, both very much part of my Jewish tradition, as were the extraordinary miracles of Elisha's mentor, the prophet Elijah.

Baba had brought back to life one who was declared dead. So too did Elisha, so also did Jesus. Baba cured people of serious illnesses, blindness and cancer and more, seeking nothing for Himself. Jesus did likewise on many occasions, requesting the healed person not to disclose the help he had received. Elisha cured a man of leprosy and refused all payment. A true healer seeks no reward other than to make the afflicted person well and whole again. I found other parallels between the Indian and Jewish heritage. I was partaking of them both.

Thus I thought about this inherited Jewish tradition and my new experiences in India. What was there within me, once adversity had struck that responded so readily to these spiritual masters? I learned that I was a direct descendant of the great 18th century teacher Rabbi Levi Yitzhak of Berditchev. Had something of that much-loved and celebrated Hasidic master rubbed off on me or come down to me across the generations? I decided to learn more about him.

Out of the Jewish and Indian teachings emerged the main religions of the world. This is a remarkable fact. Also remarkable are the bursts of spiritual energy that arose at intervals from within those traditions. The story of Sai Baba and His devotees, millions of them worldwide, whilst universal in teachings, is yet an Indian phenomenon steeped in Hindu lore and practice. Jesus quoted nothing but the Hebrew Scriptures, yet inspired millions far beyond that tradition, and still does.

In Eastern Europe, in the middle of the 18th century, there emerged one such vital spiritual impulse, almost unknown to the non-Jewish world, yet partaking of the same quality as those mentioned, and still influential world-wide today. The movement is known as Hasidism, a word derived from Hebrew implying piety, grace, and love of God, above all "the joy that scorches the heart." Its founder, known as Baal Shem Tov, literally Master of the Good Name, set Jewish hearts ablaze with fervour, in the same way that Baba inspires and illumines His devotees now.

Indeed one can compare the words, in use in both Hebrew and Sanskrit, that typify the main features of both their spiritual teachings, such as devotion to God, (devekut – bhakti), peace (shalom – shanti), indwelling spirit (ruah – atma), love (ahava – prema), holy person (tzaddik – sadhu), truth (emet – sathya), righteousness (tzedek – dharma), spiritual teacher (rabbi – guru), devotional songs in praise of God (Tehilim – Bhajans) and many more expressions that parallel one another.

Their teachings have so much in common. Enjoy the world, sing, be happy, love nature and God's creation, and come close to God with no intermediary, pray with your heart, be involved in service to others. Both Baba and Baal Shem Tov are men of God, imbued with God's Presence. The latter states, "God sees, God watches. He is in every life, in every thing. The world hinges on His Will. It is He who decides how many times the leaf will turn in the dust before the wind blows it away." Baba states, "The first requisite is faith in God. Everything we see is a manifestation of God. Wherever we are, there is God."

Indeed the Hasidic Master would have agreed wholeheartedly with Sai Baba when the latter states, "Devotion means giving up all other desires and dedicating all actions and thoughts to God. When you offer every act of yours to God, it becomes worship. Everything you do must be done as an offering to God." Those words are also the essence of the Hasidic beliefs.

Following Baal Shem Tov, who died in 1760, there came a number of inspired Hasidic Masters, among whom was one from whom I am directly descended, namely Rabbi Levi Yitzhak of Berditchev. When my grandfather Yitzhak Turgeman died in Israel in 1956 newspaper reports all mentioned his descent from the great Rabbi. My grandfather was born in Hebron in 1875, and was named after his illustrious ancestor. I could not then understand the significance of this. Now I have studied the life of my famous ancestor. So great was his spiritual reputation that one of his celebrated colleagues stated, "God is a Tzaddik (holy one) up there and Levi Yitzhak is one down here."

Levi Yitzhak was born in Galicia, Central Europe, in 1740. He was a spiritual and scholastic prodigy, but, like Baba, was totally indifferent to public opinion. And, like Baba, he never said a bad word about God's children.

There is a true story that illustrates this perfectly:

A Passover Story

No one could get Rabbi Levi Yitzhak of Berditchev angry. No matter what anyone did, he would always find something nice to say. He believed in treating all people kindly, no matter how much his patience was tested.

Rabbi Levi Yitzhak's neighbour had a son who did not want to keep any of the mitzvoth (good deeds). One year, during the Seder (Passover festive dinner), the family was about to make a 'sandwich' of matza. To everyone's surprise, the boy pulled from his pocket two slices of bread (forbidden during the Passover festival) and some meat, and made himself a sandwich. His father started to cry: "How dare you bring bread to my Seder?"

"But father," the boy answered, "I'm hungry after reading the Haggadah (religious scripture). What difference does it make if I eat bread or matza? I'm sure Rabbi Levi Yitzhak wouldn't mind. The father jumped up from the table and grabbed his son. "Oh wouldn't he? Lets go ask him." The whole family marched next door, the father leading the boy by the ear. "Rabbi," the man said, "even you would not tolerate what my

son just did. He ate bread at our Seder. I have four sons, Rabbi, and I don't have to tell you which one he is."

Everyone in the room was shocked; everyone, that is, except for Rabbi Levi Yitzhak. He smiled at the boy and asked if it was true.

"Of course, Rabbi. I was hungry so I made myself a sandwich."

"Don't you know that on Passover Jewish people don't eat bread," Rabbi Levi Yitzhak continued.

"Well, Rabbi," the boy answered, "to be totally honest, I don't really believe in all this. What difference could it possibly make if I eat bread or matza?"

The entire room was silent. Only the boy's mother could be heard sobbing in the doorway. "Please come here," Rabbi Levi Yitzhak called to the boy. The boy walked slowly, afraid that this time he had gone too far. As he approached the table, the Rabbi hugged him. "Such a fine boy," he said to the father, "and so honest too," he added to the mother. "He's ready to admit what he did and he's acting according to his beliefs. Such a fine, honest boy must sit with me at my Seder. I have so much to learn from him! Just one thing though," the Rabbi turned to the boy and said, "There'll be no sandwiches at the seder table - unless you make them with matza."

Both Baba and Levi Yitzhak exhibit a certain simplicity as well as a sense of humour. It is said of both of them that their impact on people transcended language. Their smiles were fraught with greater meaning than their sermons or speeches.

Levi Yitzhak spoke with God. He once said to God *"Without our sins, what would you do with Your pardon?"* Man's inner liberation was what he and his colleagues sought just as Baba has said, *"Very few of you desire to get from me the thing I have come to give you, namely, liberation itself."*

There were other great masters besides Levi Yitzhak, other Jewish Hasidic gurus like Rabbi Nachman of Bratzlav, who died aged 39 in 1810, but whose disciples to this day assemble at his place of death in the Ukraine every year, and when they speak of him they always use the present tense. For them he still lives. Baba and the Hasidim believed in the power of meditation, of silence, of purity of body and of mind, but essentially of love of God.

The more I studied, the more I appreciated the newspaper obituaries about my revered grandfather, and the more I understood the spirit of Levi Yitzhak that had come down to him, and from him to me. My rich inheritance from the past, combined with my present teachings from the East gave me a deeper appreciation of Baba's words as to the unity that exists within one great overall diversity.

SAYINGS OF RABBI AND THE GURU

The following are a few sayings of Rabbi Levi Yitzhak and of Sai Baba, in which you may find some elements in common.

Master of the Universe
I will sing a song to you
Where will I find you?
And where will I not find You?
Where I go, there are You
Where I stay, there are You
Only You. You only
You again and only You.

Rabbi Levi Yitzhak

ॐ

Wherever you walk I am there
Whomsoever you contact, I am
in that person.
I am in each.
From each I will respond.

You cannot see me in one place,
And miss me in another,
For I fill all space.
You cannot escape me, or
Do anything in secret.

Sathya Sai Baba

ॐ

If I have such a strong desire
For things that are ephemeral,
How much stronger should be
My desire for God, who is eternal
And the source of everlasting joy.

Rabbi Levi Yitzhak

ॐ

You must liberate yourself from
Attachment to fleeting things
And grow strong and firm
Against temptation.

Sathya Sai Baba

ॐ

It is well known that the main
Spiritual stage man has to

Reach is to be aware of his
Lowliness.

Rabbi Levi Yitzhak

ॐ

God gave you the time,
Space, cause, material, idea,
Skill, chance and fortune.
Why should you feel as
If you are the Doer?

Sathya Sai Baba

ॐ

When a man gazes at the
Brightness of the Creator,
Blessed be He, everything
Reverts to its source and man
Forgets his ego and is no
Longer aware of his selfhood
At all.

Rabbi Levi Yitzhak

ॐ

There is one thing that comes into
Man from the outside. That thing
Is the ego, which is formed by

Attachment to outside objects.
With desire for the world cut,
Ego automatically vanishes.

Sathya Sai Baba

ॐ

Just as a man's shadow does whatever
He does, so the Creator, blessed be He,
Does, as it were, whatever man does.
Consequently, a man must perform
Good deeds, giving alms and
Showing compassion to the needy, so
That the Creator, blessed be He, too,
Will bestow His goodness.

Rabbi Levi Yitzhak

ॐ

Service – the utilization of time and
Skill to the upliftment of society –
That is the highest form of
Adoration which God will reward
With Grace.
The service of man is the only means
By which you can serve God.
Service to man is service to God.

Sathya Sai Baba

ॐ

Man must criticize himself
And praise his fellow man.

Rabbi Levi Yitzhak

ॐ

Criticizing others, finding fault
With them – all this comes out
Of egoism. Search for your own
Faults instead and correct them.

Sathya Sai Baba

ॐ

He had no illusions about men.
Yet he loved even the most
Sinful and ignorant among
Them.

Rabbi Louis Jacobs about Rabbi Levi Yitzhak

ॐ

Never call yourself a sinner,
That kind of self condemnation
Ill becomes a child of God

Sathya Sai Baba

ॐ

When you take one step towards
God, God takes ten toward you

Sathya Sai Baba

ॐ

Let the different faiths exist,.let
Them flourish and let the glory of
God be sung in all the languages
In a variety of tunes.

Sathya Sai Baba

ॐ

SAYINGS OF SATHYA SAI BABA

(Gems of Wisdom from Sai Baba)

When writing about Baba, it is like trying to put the whole ocean into a cup. Here is just a drop from that ocean:

On Himself

I have come to light the lamp of Love in your hearts, to see that it shines day by day with added lustre. I have not come to speak on behalf of any exclusive religion. I have not come on any mission of publicity for any sect or creed or cause, nor have I come to collect followers for any doctrine. I have no plan to attract disciples or devotees into my fold or any fold. I have come to tell you of this unitary faith, this spiritual principle, this path of Love, this virtue of Love, this duty of Love, this obligation to Love.

ॐ

In this Avatar,
the wicked will not be destroyed
they will be corrected

reformed and educated
and led back to the path
from which they had strayed.

On Love

The Lord will accept a heart without words,

But he will not accept words without a heart.

ॐ

Love is patient and kind, it is not jealous or conceited or proud. Love is not ill-mannered or selfish or irritable. Love does not keep a record of wrongs. Love is not happy with evil, but is happy with truth. Love never gives up but gives faith and hope. Love is eternal.

ॐ

Love as thought is truth
Love as action is right conduct
Love as feeling is peace
Love as understanding is non-violence.

ॐ

It is enough to cultivate
the love that knows no
distinction between oneself and another – because all
are limbs of the one body
of Almighty God.

ॐ

My love shall I give
even if you do not ask
for it is your right
to share in it.

ॐ

Start the day with Love
Spend the day with Love
Fill the day with Love
End the day with Love
That is the way to God.

ॐ

I do not want your devotion
I want your transformation.

ॐ

A heart with compassion
is the Temple of God.

ॐ

Love is selflessness
Self is lovelessness.

ॐ

On Service

Ego lives
by getting and forgetting.
Love lives
by giving and forgiving.

ॐ

Service to man is service to God.

ॐ

Hands that serve are
holier than lips that pray.

ॐ

The fulfilment of human life
consists in the sevice man
renders in a spirit of selflessness.

On Happiness

My only desire is your happiness
Your happiness is my happiness
I have no happiness apart from yours.

ॐ

There is no happiness
greater than contentment.

ॐ

Take as much bliss
as you can from me
and leave me with all
your sorrows.

ॐ

I am happiest when a person
carrying a heavy load of misery
comes to me. For he is most in
need of what I have to give.

ॐ

Happiness lies not in doing what you like,
but in liking what you have to do.

On Education

Education without character
science without compassion
and commerce without morality
are useless and dangerous.

ॐ

The purpose of education
is to learn how to live
not how to make a living.

ॐ

It is said virtue is the sign
of the educated person,
the thing which makes
education worthwhile.

ॐ

The end of education is character.

ॐ

On Suffering

Why worry when God in order to make a lovely jewel of you,
heats and melts, cuts and carves, and removes your dross
in the crucible of sufferings.

ॐ

Further Sayings

Be what you profess to be
speak what you intend to do,
utter what you have experienced,
no more, no less.

ॐ

I give you what you want
so that you may want
what I have come to give you,
the Love of God.

ॐ

Do not cage God
in a picture-frame.
Do not confine Him
In an idol.
He is all forms.
He is all names.

ॐ

Right is right
even if nobody does it.
And wrong is wrong
Even if everybody does it.

ॐ

When the sun is over your head there will be no shadow,
similarly when faith is steady in your head,
it should not cast any shadow of doubt.

ॐ

Tolerate all kinds of persons and opinions all attitudes and peculiarities. The school, the home and the society are all training grounds for tolerance.

ॐ

Never give up God,
holding Him responsible for your ills,
believe rather that the ills
draw you closer to God.

ॐ

Where there is faith – there is Love
Where there is Love – there is peace
Where there is peace – there is truth
Where there is truth – there is bliss
Where there is bliss – there is God.

ॐ

Take one step towards me
I shall take a hundred towards you.
Shed but one tear,
I shall wipe away a hundred from your eyes.

ॐ

Miracles are not part of my personality
but only a token of my Love.

ॐ

Help ever
Hurt never.

ॐ

A virtuous character
is our only lasting possession.

ॐ

To the doubting or confused ones, I give this illustration. Those who want to secure pearls from the sea have to dive deep to fetch them. It does not help them to dabble among the shallow waves near the shore and say that the sea has no pearls and all stories about them are false.

ॐ

Follow the master,
face the devil,
fight to the end,
and finish the game.

ॐ

Science is the study of the creation;
spirituality is the study of the Creator.

ॐ

THE ANGEL

I call him an 'Angel'. Without him I could not have made any progress with this book. I was told he was going to Baba's ashram, to stay there for an indefinite time. We both worked as volunteers in a Sai Baba bookshop in London. He was very computer literate and had just joined us in assisting with the book shop computer related tasks. I hardly knew him, having merely exchanged a few words when I saw him at the shop on one or two occasions.

At that time I had just purchased a computer, but found it difficult to work. I was frustrated and wondered who could help me get my manuscript typed using the computer. One Friday morning I had a phone call. It was this 'Angel' offering to come and help me with formulating the manuscript on the computer.

I could not believe my ears. I asked him how come he had returned from India so soon (hardly a week after he left). He related to me the story when he came to my house. Apparently every time he attended Darshan and Baba appeared, he received a message in his mind saying, "go back home, there is work for you to do there". This puzzled him. The following day he went into the ashram book shop just to browse around. He picked up a book and opened a page at random. What he read confirmed to him the message Baba was giving him at Darshan. In the book he picked up, the author was relating an interview that he had with Baba when he asked Baba that he wished to remain in the ashram to be near Him. Baba answered saying, "Go back home as there is still work for you to do there!" Reading this, his message was confirmed and he promptly booked his return ticket. After arriving back home, a day or two later he came into the book shop in London. As soon as he entered through the door one of the volunteers said to him, "Phone Ruth, she needs help with her computer". He did so immediately and came to help me and put all I have written onto the computer. His help was extraordinarily timely and invaluable.

How amazing are Baba's ways to assist his devotees!

This 'Angel', who wished to remain anonymous, was inspired to write the following after reading my manuscript:

For my Dearest Ruth

Beneath the calm waves of the ocean, an oyster rested in her shell upon a coral bank. The oyster was deeply troubled for she had been feeling a pain deep within her. She glanced around her world and felt lonely as she watched the other beings playing and talking with each other, wrapped up in their lives. How the oyster wished to be with them. She had been like them once, but now her pain was so great that she remained for days attached to the coral feeling lost and hurt.

As time passed, a beautiful dolphin swam by. Seeing the oyster and recognising her pain, he spoke "Why are you upset, little one?"

"I have a pain inside me", said the oyster. She thought it was quite unusual to see a dolphin in this part of the ocean, but was not afraid of him. The dolphin laughed playfully and spoke again. "My most precious beloved friend, do not worry about the other creatures, or feel remorse about what you once had and have now lost. I have come to share with you the greatest secret. The pain you feel within you is a pearl of great beauty...."

In God's Love

SAI BABA AND HIS MESSAGE

A Final Summary

You have read of Sai Baba in his role as educator, healer, and spiritual leader, social worker. Thousands of people in every country in the world are witnesses to these aspects of Baba's life and work.

Those followers are not members of a sect or cult, but people from all walks of life, races, cultural backgrounds and religions. For Baba encourages us to seek the underlying unity and divinity in ourselves, in others and in our lives. He states: -

"There is only one religion, the reiigion of Love,
There is only one language, the language of the Heart,
There is only one caste, the caste of Humanity,
There is only one God and He is Omnipresent".

Baba inspires not only through His teaching but also above all through His example. He lives frugally and renders ceaseless service to those around Him, making Himself approachable and available to thousand daily, while maintaining a tireless programme of lecturing, administering, writing, encouraging the students. He has no secretary, cleans His own room, accepts no money from anyone (indeed fund-raising is forbidden throughout the organisation).

His manner is always patient, gentle, gracious, often humorous and playful. Although invited countless times to visit other countries, Baba has so far remained in India, (apart from one visit to Africa) maintaining that one has to put one's own house in order before advising others.

His birthplace, once a tiny rural village, is now a beautiful university town with schools and colleges lining its main street. In addition, hundreds of villages in surrounding areas have been adopted by Baba's voluntary workers who have built roads, bridges, and schools and dug wells for them. Regular medical camps care for the health of thousands of local people and Baba's Education programme has been implemented in schools throughout India and other countries. His **E**ducation in **H**uman **V**alues (EHV) programme has been adapted in many parts of the world, including 80 schools in Britain. It has had a marked effect on children, resulting in a dramatic fall in violence, drug taking and crime.

Again it is not only His example, which inspires but also His extraordinary level of being, which shines through His teachings and has an impact on all who come into His Presence.

His frequently witnessed and documented healings, materialisations of objects, telepathic powers and appearances in more than one place at the same time are due to powers He was born with, not developed by special disciplines. It is said He is not just a fully realised man but also the Main Spiritual Leader of this Age; His life certainly fulfils prophecies in several religions. He says:

"I know who I am;
I have come to help you realise who you are".

What are we to make of all this? Could a man, who left his village school at the age of thirteen, have such a profound knowledge of the world religions and the ability to teach and explain them with sayings and stories of Christ-like simplicity? Baba says: -

"Come, test, inquire
taste, experience".

He also says:

"...do not be attracted simply by stories of what I create by a wave of the hand. Do not jump to conclusions with closed eyes; watch, study and weigh.."

Since 1950, Sathya Sai Baba's residence and headquarters have been in Prasanthi Nilayam (the Abode of Supreme Peace), a parcel of land adjacent to the village. His name spread quickly in India, and then He became known to people on every Continent. For many years Prasanthi Nilayam has been a gathering site for millions of spiritual pilgrims, from all religions, throughout the world.

In the 1990s, a huge Super Speciality Hospital had been built near Prasanthi Nilayam giving free medical treatment to the poor, and more recently a massive Water Project bringing clean drinking water to over 800 drought-stricken villages. In 2000, another splendid hospital was built, in Bangalore, a service without payment for all who come.

Sai Baba sums up His mission in these words:-

"Whenever disharmony overwhelms the world
The Lord will incarnate in human form to establish the modes of earning peace, and to re-educate the human community in the paths of peace.

The fame of Sathya Sai Baba was spread, in the beginning, by the stories of His 'miracles', acts which cannot be explained by science and which transcend physical laws. His manifestation of material objects, the creation of sacred ash (vibhuti) on the palm and fingers of His right hand, to be used for spiritual and physical aid, changing an object from one metal to another metal simply by blowing on it, all of these and many more, before hundreds of thousands of people, all done "by an act of will".

He is known to heal the sick, the maimed, the blind; He has protected from harm those who called for help, even though thousands of miles away, He has appeared in His physical form in two different places at the same time, and He has raised from the dead several persons. And yet, He states,

"You have come to get from Me tinsel and trash, the petty cures and promotions, worldly toys and comforts. Very few of you desire to get from Me the thing I have come to give you, namely, liberation itself."

It has been said His greatest miracles are the transformation of people who come to Him, often with doubts and apprehension, and who leave with love in their hearts, peace in their minds, and a resolve to live a more useful, spiritual life.

I would like to add here just two quotes from the numerous eminent people who have been convinced of Baba's Divinity. First, Dr. S. Bhagavatham, India's leading nuclear physicist said to the Indian Ministry of Defence:

"He transcends the known laws of physics and chemistry. I have therefore to declare this man a transcendental being, divine."

Second, Dr. V.K Gokak Oxford-educated intellectual, writer, poet, educationist, and until recently the head of Sai Baba's University at Puttaparthi said of Baba:

"He is a Cosmic Visitor".

Lessons for Mankind by Sai Baba

Since Sai Baba is a Divine Incarnation (a Poorna Avatar) with full powers to change the world in the 'twinkling of an eye', He is at times asked by His devotees why He allows so much suffering and disasters and does not make the world a more peaceful and happier place?

Baba explains that it is never the task of a Redeemer to resolve human errors with a magic wand. Doing so would ensure that the errors would continue to be committed and man would find himself in the same situation again.

This is why He has incarnated, to teach humanity His five precepts of Love, Peace, Righteousness, Truth and Non-violence. Man has to change his negative and destructive thoughts and find peace within himself, and then there will be peace in society and in the world. Unfortunately, man has to learn these lessons by his own mistakes and sufferings".

Sanathana Sarathi Magazine, May 1994

IN LIGHTER MOOD

They say that laughter is the best medicine, so maybe the following will raise a smile as you conclude this book.

The tongue weighs practically nothing,
but so few people can hold it.

☺ ☺ ☺

Learn from others' mistakes.
You can't live long enough to make them all yourself.

☺ ☺ ☺

Great minds discuss ideas.
Average minds discuss events,
Small minds discuss people.

☺ ☺ ☺

If you can spend a perfectly useless afternoon in a perfectly useless manner, you have learned to live.

Lin Yutang

☺ ☺ ☺

The past is history.
The future a mystery.
That is why this moment is a gift
and is called the present.

(with thanks to Michael Man Centre)

☺ ☺ ☺

God and Man

A young man once asked God how long a million years was to Him.

God replied ***"A million years to Me is just like a single second in your time".***

Then the young man asked God what a million dollars was to Him.
God replied, ***"A million dollars to Me is just like a single penny to you".***

Then the young man got up his courage and asked, ***"God, could I have one of your pennies?"***

God smiled and replied, ***"Certainly, just a second".***

(With thanks to Dr. Eli Gersten and the Jewish Association of Spiritual Healers)

☺ ☺ ☺

May Love, Light and Peace

Enter the Heart of all Mankind.

Love All Serve All

-Baba

BOOKS TO READ

The Grace and Blessings I have received from Baba will forever be cherished in my heart, but also I must say that His infinite love and blessings are things most, if not all, devotees have experienced in one way or another.

I have heard the most amazing stories and experiences from so many devotees over the years, which would fill volumes. This truly is a bond and a source of comfort to us all. There are a great many books written with accounts of these extraordinary experiences, which make for fascinating and uplifting reading. I present here a list of books that have inspired my heart and mind.

- **Sai Baba Man of Miracles,** Howard Murphet, Frederick Muller Limited, 1971 *(Has inspired many go to see Baba for themselves)*
- **Sai Baba The Holy Man and the Psychiatrist,** Samuel Sandweiss M.D., Birth Day Publishing, 1975 *(A very influential book)*
- **My Baba and I**, Dr. J. Hislop, Sri Sathya Sai Books and Publications Trust.
- **Sathya Sai Baba, The Embodiment of Love,** Peggy Mason and Ron Laing, Pilgrim Books, 1982

- **Pathway to God,** Jonathan Roof, Leela Press, 1991
- **Vision of Sai,** Rita Bruce, Sri Sathya Sai Books and Publications Trust.
- **Loving God,** Professor N. Kasturi, Sri Sathya Sai Books and Publications Trust.
- **Sai Baba The Ultimate Experience,** Phyllis Krystal, Sri Sathya Sai Books and Publications Trust.
- **Inspired Medicine – Sathya Sai Baba's Influence in Medical Practice,** Compiled and edited by Judy Warner. Leela Press 2000
- **Gems of Wisdom – Quotations from Bhagawan Sri Sathya Sai Baba**
- **Miracles are my Visiting Cards,** Erlendur Haraldsson, PhD, Sai Towers Publishing
- **The Secret Path,** Dr. Paul Brunton, Rider and Company
- **A Message from Arunachala,** Dr. Paul Brunton, Rider and Company, 1936
- **Everyman's Goal,** Rebecca Beard, Arthur James Publishing, 1952
- **Autobiography of a Yogi,** by Paramahansa Yogananda.
- **The Divine Romance,** Paramahansa Yoganda, Self-Realisation Fellowship, 1972
- **Man's Eternal Quest**, Paramahansa Yogananda, Self-Realisation Fellowship. 1973

- **A Soul's Journey**. Peter Riccheliey, Turnstone Books, 1972
- **Somebody Loves You,** Helen Steiner Rice, Hutchinson and Co., 1976.

An excellent source of literature, videos, photographs, music and sundries regarding Sai Baba can be found at the following addresses:

Central London (UK)

Sri Sathya Sai Organisation
16 Melcombe Street
London NW1 6AH
0207 723 5500
(Please send a stamped self addressed envelope to this address for a full price list)

Tel: +44 (0) 181 732 2886
Fax: +44 (0) 181 909 3954
Email: saibooks@btinernet.com/-saibooks
Internet: http://www.srisathyasai.org.in/

For information on groups and centres within the UK please contact: -
Mr. Roy Creek,
Information Officer,
Sai Baba Organisation,
Telephone: 01923 720 709

IN GRATITUDE

I am privileged to have such valued friends in Aubrey and Sheila Rose. I feel deeply grateful to Aubrey for giving so much of his precious time and talent to edit this book with such understanding and perception. Equally I am so grateful to Sheila for all her patience and dedication in typing and re-typing the whole of the manuscript.

I have to acknowledge that without Aubrey's painstaking help in editing my manuscript this book would not have seen the light of day.